THERE'S HOPE
for the
FUTURE

THERE'S HOPE

for the

FUTURE

You Can Look Forward Confidently to What's Ahead Because God's Promises Are Sure

RICHARD G. LEE

BROADMAN
& HOLMAN
PUBLISHERS

Nashville, Tennessee

© 1996 by Richard Lee

Printed in the United States of America

4261-88
0-8054-6188-4

Published by
Broadman & Holman Publishers
Nashville, Tennessee

Design: Steven Boyd

Dewey Decimal Classification: 248
Subject Heading: Christian Life
Library of Congress Card Catalog Number: 95-572

Unless otherwise stated, all Scripture quotations are from the King James Version of the Bible. Those marked TLB are from The Living Bible, copyright © Tyndale House Publishers, Wheaton, Ill., 1971, used by permission.

Library of Congress Cataloging-in-Publication Data
Lee, Richard, 1946–
      There's hope for the future / Richard Lee.
          p. cm.
      Includes bibliographical references.
      ISBN 0-8054-6188-4 (hardback)
      1. Christian life. 2. Christianity—Forecasting. 3. Hope—Religious aspects—Christianity. I. Title.
  BV4501.2.L42535   1996
  270.8—dc20   95-572
                                                         CIP

00 99 98 97 96 5 4 3 2 1

This book is dedicated to
the children and youth of Rehoboth Church,
whose very presence assures their pastor
there is indeed hope for the future.

Contents

Preface

I'm excited about the future! The days ahead are going to be the greatest days the world has ever known. They will not be without their problems or challenges. But they will be days of incredible opportunity in every area of life.

Advances in technology and medicine will increase the quality of our lives. The growth of the global economy will benefit nearly everyone of us directly. Improved communications will bring the whole world to our personal doorstep. People will go more places, do more things, and live better than they ever have before.

I am not a pessimist about the future, but I am a *realist*. All these improvements can only enhance our temporal lives. They cannot provide the fundamental meaning of life itself. Only God can do that! Times may change but He never changes. Fads may come and go, but human nature remains the same. People need help, love, forgiveness, and hope.

The future does not have to be dark and gloomy. The changes and challenges that lie ahead are God-given opportunities for us to live our lives in accordance with His will and purpose. The future is not something to be shunned, but embraced; it brings us one step closer to God.

This is a book of joy, excitement, and hope for the future. It will reflect on the past, examine the present, and speculate on the future. It will inform, challenge, motivate, and help you as you face your own personal future. It will also encourage you to face the future with confidence—knowing that God is in control!

Dealing with the future involves seeing tomorrow's possibilities in light of today's realities—today is the gateway to tomorrow. The decisions you make today will determine what you become tomorrow. The course of the future will be set by the sails of today. Now is the time to see what is coming and determine how best to handle it—to the glory of God.

My heartfelt thanks and appreciation to Dr. Ed Hindson, vice president of *There's Hope!*, for his editorial advice and assistance, and to Mrs. Emily Boothe for typing the original draft of this manuscript. Their daily assistance in our broadcast ministry is a great help to me. Gratitude is also expressed to Dr. David Self for his helpful insights, and the Lord's servants at Broadman & Holman Publishers; Chuck Wilson, Bucky Rosenbaum, Greg Webster, and Vicki Crumpton.

And loving appreciation to my darling wife, Judy, mother of our two children, Jason and Tonya, who helps me be reminded each day that there is indeed hope for the future!

Part 1

Making the Most
of Your Future

1

Keys to the Future

The future will be here before you know it!" my dad once told me. *Maybe,* I thought as a young man, *but the future is a long way off.* Well, time has come and gone, and guess what? Dad was right! The future came a lot sooner than I ever expected.

Almost everybody is interested in the future, but few people can see the future with any real clarity. Over the years, I have listened to many prognostications about future events, and most of them never worked out the way they were supposed to.

But there was at least one man whose understanding of the future was right on target. He had such a thorough grasp of the trends of his time that he was able to project a very accurate view of our world today.

In 1976, Francis Schaeffer wrote his provocative book *How Shall We Then Live?*[1] In it, he outlined the rise and fall of Western culture. Schaeffer carefully laid the backdrop to modern society. Then he raised his concerns as to where it was headed—love without meaning, murder without guilt, education without truth, wealth without purpose.

Schaeffer foresaw the world of the future. Though his book is now more than twenty years old, it is as up-to-date as the morning paper. The widespread use of drugs, abortion on demand, euthanasia, genetic manipulation, uncontrollable crime, the basic disintegration of law and morality—all clearly predicted. In general, he foresaw a society without God. A society suffering the consequences of its own selfish indulgence.

In many ways, Schaeffer was right. But despite the gloom and doom of secular society—which we see televised into our living rooms every day—there is also a parallel trend in the opposite direction. It is a ray of hope in a society gone mad. It is a shining beacon of light on the rocky shores of a troubled society.

It is the simple fact that God is not dead. He is still very much alive! He is at work in His people everywhere, creating hope in spite of hopelessness, light in the darkness, and love in the emptiness of human life.

This is a time of great opportunity for the people of God. The greater the darkness, the more powerfully the light of truth shines. The greater the despair, the more glorious the hope.

It was my privilege to host the All Media Breakfast at the National Religious Broadcasters Convention in Nashville in February 1995. At that breakfast, D. James Kennedy, senior minister of the Coral Ridge Presbyterian Church in Ft. Lauderdale, Florida, made these startling and encouraging observations based on statistics from the Center for World Missions in California:

- In A.D. 100 there were 100 converts to Christ per day worldwide.
- In 1900 the number of converts to Christ had grown to 943 per day.
- In 1950 the number had grown to 4,500 per day.
- By 1980 the number of converts accelerated to 20,000 per day.
- In 1995 that number jumped to more than 90,000 per day.

Dr. Kennedy speculated that there could well be over 200,000 converts to Christ per day by the year 2000! He also observed that the National Research exit polls indicates a growing number of professing "evangelical born-again" Christians participating in our national elections.

- 1988—18 percent of the voters claimed to be born-again believers.
- 1992—24 percent of the voters claimed to be born-again believers.
- 1994—33 percent of the voters claimed to be born-again believers.

If these statistics are accurate, that means that born-again believers are the largest single voting bloc in the American electorate. That fact alone ought to give us hope for the future.

Movie critic Ted Baer believes that the anti-Christian bias in Hollywood film making reached a peak in 1987 with *The Last Temptation of Christ*. That year, there were ninety movies bashing Christians. By 1994 that number had dropped to only seven such films. During the same period, the number of family films has risen from six per year to seventy-five such films produced last year. Many of them were top box office attractions.

This is a time of great opportunity for the people of God. The greater the darkness, the more powerfully the light of truth shines. The greater the despair, the more glorious the hope.

Things seem to be changing. I believe we are living in tremendous times. Ahead are perhaps the greatest days the world has ever known. We now have at our disposal the greatest tools of communication man has ever devised. You can sit in your own living room with a cellular phone, a fax machine, a computer, and a modem and communicate with the entire world.

We live in a "fax-it-to-me" and "fly-it-to-me" world. Anything and everything is possible. We have the technology to do in a moment what our ancestors could only dream about. But all that technology is useless, if we don't have a reason to use it.

Full Speed Ahead . . . to Nowhere

Modern man has reduced months of travel to a few hours. Hours of labor have been cut to milliseconds of time. We can go more places, do more things, and accomplish more results than any generation that has ever lived. Yet public surveys continue to reveal that ours is an unhappy and unfulfilled generation.[2]

A recent issue of *Time* magazine ran a special feature entitled "Beyond the Year 2000: What to Expect in the New Millennium."[3] The article on the family predicted a society of house-husbands, working mothers, and latch-key children. It went on to predict the possibility of unwanted, victimized children roaming the streets like they are today in South America. The traditional family will be replaced by "serial monogamy" (multiple marriages). As marriage and families are terminated, traditional morality will collapse. *Time's* feature does not paint a pretty picture of the future.

People are spending less time with family and friends. They are less satisfied with their personal lives. And they are less fulfilled with their work, their possessions, and their immediate circumstances. The trend is even worse among younger adults ("Baby Busters").

Moody magazine observes that the "Busters" (also called "Generation X," or "Twenty-Somethings") are struggling with a world of busted dreams. They view everything through the disillusionment of their own lives: the environment is busted, the economy is busted, marriage is busted, and even the sexual revolution is busted (with AIDS). In her insightful article, Jan Johnson observes, "More than half of all baby busters were raised in divorced or blended families. Now that they are adults they feel estranged from family, community, God, and even self."[4]

It is obvious that we have our work cut out for us. If middle-aged America is going to raise any element of hope for the younger generation, it must be now. And it must be based upon honesty and reality, not hyped up emotion, empty rhetoric, or broken promises. Real hope from real people is what this generation wants and demands.

Finding Hope for the Future

Pessimists always see the dark side of life. They focus on the problems and the difficulties. They rarely see the positive options or solutions to life's problems. On the other hand, *idealists* tend to oversimplify the solutions. Everything will be fine. Don't worry. Lighten up. They've got great slogans, but few solutions. *Realists,* by contrast, see the problems, but are willing to devise a plan of action to correct them.

> But a balanced perspective maximizes the negatives and positives of life. I prefer to call such a perspective realistic optimism.

The real key for all of us is balance. It is the extremes that keep us out of balance in life. But a balanced perspective maximizes the negatives and positives of life. I prefer to call such a perspective *realistic optimism.*

Some people can rush ahead foolishly without being properly prepared. The future belongs to those who prepare for it. Also realize that there are those whose dreams are so far beyond their ability to produce, that they are little more than vain visions of unrealistic expectations.

But for most of us, this is not the problem! The real problem is our inability to trust God to help us overcome our fear of the future. I am convinced there are positive and negative consequences to all of our actions. If you eat too much, you'll gain weight. If you eat too little, you're liable to starve to death. But in either case, there are consequences to our actions.

Realistic optimism faces those problems honestly and directly. It helps us keep a positive focus on negative issues. It also helps us to focus on the major issues, rather than the minor ones. And, above all, it encourages us to find solutions to the problems of life. Realistic optimism would rather light a candle than curse the darkness. It would rather embrace the future than run from it.

The future does not have to overwhelm us, nor does it have to scare us. Certainly it will have its challenges and difficulties. But if we can see where we are going, and figure out how to get there, the rest will be easy.

Making the Most of Your Future

We all need to learn the lessons of history as well as the lessons of our own personal past. But the key to life is learning to live effectively in the present. Today's decisions will become tomorrow's realities. Once we learn to make the right decisions today, we can leap into the future with faith and confidence.

> *Over the years, God has enabled me to focus on "three keys" that have helped me deal with the future.*

Over the years, God has enabled me to focus on "three keys" that have helped me deal with the future. Once you understand *what* they are and *how* to use them, I believe they could revolutionize your life. They will keep you from being bound by past failures and limitations. They will also prevent you from running ahead foolishly.

Some people never move ahead effectively because they are prisoners of their past failures. They are afraid to make decisions and commitments or take steps of action for fear they will make another mistake. Let me assure you that you don't have to be imprisoned by your past. God is the God of the second chance. He will make a way for you to start over again.

Other people plunge ahead foolishly without counting the cost. They don't learn from their past mistakes, so they are doomed to repeat them again. Until we understand what God is trying to tell us by our decisions, we won't make better ones. Learning from our mistakes can help us make better choices in the future.

Here is the pattern God has shown me about dealing with the future:

| LEARN FROM THE PAST |
| LIVE IN THE PRESENT |
| LEAP INTO THE FUTURE |

Another way to express these concepts would be to "Look Back," reflect on the past; "Look Out," deal with the present; and "Look Ahead," focus on the future consequences of your present actions.

"That's obvious!" someone will say. "Then why aren't you doing it?" I would reply. It is the simple concepts that are the most profound—and the most helpful. These are the basic truths that help us understand how to live. And how to live *effectively*.

We all need to learn the lessons of the *past*. The mistakes we made yesterday will help us learn to make better decisions tomorrow.

The key to effective living is learning to live in the *present*. Today's decisions will become tomorrow's realities. They will be the foundation stones on which we can build a better and more effective future. If I were building a house, I would illustrate it like this:

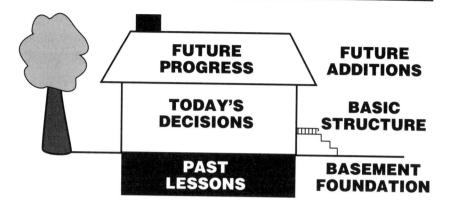

Once the superstructure is in place, you can move ahead with faith and confidence. You have something on which to build your life and family. Leaping into the future is a leap of confidence. It is not a blind leap into the dark. Rather, it is a step of confidence based on past experiences. Once you learn to handle the past, you will be ready to tackle the future.

Priority of the Present

The hinge on which these three keys work is the *present*. What we do today determines what will happen in the future. This is not to suggest that God cannot intervene dramatically in our circumstances. He certainly can! But more often than not, our future success depends on our present actions.

Let me illustrate this is several ways: Bill is hurt by a decision made by his boss at work. His hurt quickly turns to bitterness. If Bill doesn't deal with that bitterness, he will start making every decision in his life based upon that bitterness. It won't be long until the bitterness affects his life, his job, his family, and his future.

By the same token, Donna is told she is being transferred to another office across town. Instead of feeling threatened by this move, she looks upon it as a promotion. She shows up at the new location with a positive spirit and is immediately welcomed and accepted at her new location.

What determined these future outcomes? Past evaluation and present action. Negative attitudes led to negative actions. Positive attitudes led to positive actions. Donna succeeded where Bill failed because she made the most of her challenge.

Priorities determine actions. Actions shape the present. And the present determines the future:

Priorities

⇩

Present Actions

⇩

Future Consequences

Tom Jackson was a successful businessman in Atlanta. When he joined our church, he was at the height of his career with Southern Bell. But Tom was worried to death about the future. He never seemed able to enjoy his life, family, or career.

"Downsizing! Cutbacks! Layoffs!" he would thunder. "One of these days, I'll be the one they let go!"

Tom worried about everything: collapse of the economy, the possible bankruptcy of Social Security, the inability of medical technology, rising costs, plummeting dollars, the national deficit. On and on.

"Tom," I asked him sternly one day, "where is God in all this?"

"What do you mean?" he asked. "I go to church."

"That's not my point, Tom," I replied. "Where is God's priority, plan, and peace in your life?"

He glanced down and sat speechless.

"If you were as concerned about God as you are about all these other things, you'd get a better focus on the future," I reminded him.

Jesus taught the very same concepts in the Sermon on the Mount. He said, "But seek ye first the kingdom of God, and his righteousness; and all these things shall be added unto you" (Matt. 6:33).

What was our Lord talking about? Priorities! And spiritual priorities at that! He was reminding all of us that we must put first things first in our lives. Ultimately, God must be first. When He is, all other relationships and decisions will fall into their proper places.

Technological advances, new strategies, and better methods will never take the place of God in your life. All the "progress" we have made in the past century has only left us more isolated and insecure as a society. More than ever before, we need to be loved, accepted, and understood. No one can do that for you any better than God Himself!

> *More than ever before, we need to be loved, accepted, and understood.*

He loves you with a love that is greater than your sin. He forgives you with a grace that is more sufficient than your unbelief. And He accepts you as His child with a compassion that goes beyond human comprehension.

Putting It All Together

"My past is such a mess," one of my friends confessed. "Richard, you cannot imagine how terrible I feel," he added. "Is there any hope for me?"

"Yes, there is!" I could tell him with confidence. Why? Because I was convinced that God was still in the business of forgiving sinners, reclaiming failures, and transforming lives. You don't have to remain the victim of your past—constantly doubting, struggling, wondering. Bring it all to the altar of grace. God will receive you by faith.

You don't have to remain frozen in the present, incapable of moving ahead. God can change your heart and turn it toward Him. He can remove those present barriers and set you free to live for Him. In short, He can give you a glorious future—if you will let Him. Don't underestimate His power. He can do for you what you cannot do for yourself. He can make all the difference in your life—both now and in the future.

We live on the verge of a brand new century. Indeed, a brand new millennium. The twenty-first century is upon us. The third millennium is just around the corner. Challenges? Yes. Changes? Yes. Confusion? No!

Christ is the *same* yesterday, today, and forever. He is the anchor of our souls, the foundation of our lives, and the hope of our future. Trust Him to forgive your past, direct your present, and mold your future.

Your life is in His hands. He makes no mistakes! Trust Him to unfold your future with joy and confidence. Leap ahead by faith and action. Put God first in your life, and He will bless the results.

Focus on the Future

1. How is the world changing, and how do those changes affect you personally?

   _____

   _____

   _____

2. What is *realistic optimism?*

   _____

   _____

   _____

3. How can you balance excessive optimism or pessimism?

   _____

   _____

   _____

4. Using the "three keys," evaluate where you've been, where you are, and where you want to go.

   _____

   _____

   _____

Three Keys	My Response
Learn from the Past	
Live in the Present	
Leap into the Future	

2

Laying Hold of God's Promises

When I was a boy, I tended to believe almost everything people told me. If someone made me a promise, I just assumed that they meant to keep it. As I grew older, I learned that not every promise could be trusted or taken seriously. Someone might casually promise me something, but unfortunately they had little intention of ever actually doing it. Just recently I asked a repairman who had broken a promise why he had done it. His reply was, "Well, I guess I'm just human." He was right. We humans have a way of breaking promises and letting folks down.

Unlike human promises, the promises of God can be trusted with absolute confidence. You and I need never worry about whether or not God intends to fulfill His promises. The apostle Peter said, "The Lord is not slack concerning his promise" (2 Pet. 3:9). Peter was right. Again and again the Bible assures us that what God said He would do, He will do!

Whenever I think of biblical promises, I am reminded of the story found in the early chapters of the Book of Joshua where God promised to make Joshua victorious and give the land of Canaan to the people of Israel.

No people ever faced greater obstacles than did the Israelites in the Old Testament. They had been in bondage in Egypt for four hundred years. Even after their miraculous crossing of the Red Sea and their deliverance from the Egyptians, they had spent an additional forty years wandering in the wilderness of Sinai. For all those years they had tenaciously clung to the promise that God had made to their forefather, Abraham: He would give the land of Canaan to his descendants. They knew that this promised land "flowed with milk and honey," and that it was all that they had ever heard it was and more than enough to meet their needs.

As the children of Israel followed Joshua through the wilderness to the outskirts of the promised land, they faced two immediate obstacles. First, the Jordan River, which served as a natural boundary between them and the land of Canaan, was flooded over its banks as they approached it. Second, the mighty Canaanites and several other tribes of people occupied the various parts of that land, and they were not about to relinquish it without a fight. These obstacles, however, were insignificant in light of the promise of God. The Lord had said unto Joshua, "Every place that the sole of your foot shall tread upon, that have I given unto you" (Josh. 1:3). God had named the borders of Israel which would extend from Lebanon in the north to Egypt in the south, and from the Mediterranean on the west to the Euphrates River on the east. He further promised Joshua that none of the people of the land of Canaan would be able to stand before him if he would meditate on His Word day and night and obey all that He commanded him to do. With the promise of God before him, and the power of God within him, Joshua marched forward in victorious obedience.

Promises, Plans, and Power

God's promises are always made in accordance with His plans for us. And it is only to the degree that we lay hold of His promises that we will see the plan and purpose of God unfolded in our lives. It is also to this degree that we will see the power of God at work on our behalf. These three Ps all work simultaneously: Promises, Plans, and Power. As we believe the promises of God, and act upon the plan of God, we will always experience the power of God in our lives.

To reinforce His promise to Joshua, the Lord commanded him to bring the people of Israel to the banks of the Jordan River. When they arrived, they found the river overflowing its banks, making it all but impossible to cross. In order to focus their attention on God Himself, the Lord told Joshua to command the priests to carry the ark of the covenant into the Jordan River. (The ark of the covenant was the place where the blood of sacrifice was applied to the mercy seat and where the glory of God resided among the Israelites. In essence, the ark of the covenant symbolized God's power and presence with His people.) The Scriptures tell us that the priests carried the ark into the river, and as the soles of their feet rested in the waters of the Jordan, the Israelites were able to cross over on dry land!

Just as Moses had miraculously led the children of Israel across the Red Sea at the beginning of their journey, now Joshua led them miraculously across the Jordan River at the end of their journey. In all, it had been a journey of faith. For some, it had been a very difficult time in which hard lessons had to be learned. In fact, a whole generation had been lost in the wilderness. But now the people were ready to believe God and to obey His word. As they followed the ark of the covenant across the Jordan River, they knew that they could trust the promises of God because they were beginning to see them fulfilled. A covenant is an agreement or a promise. The ark of the covenant also represented the fulfillment of God's promises to His people. As the Israelites watched the ark of promise being taken across the river, their own faith in the promises of God was being strengthened.

Keep Your Eyes on the Goal

There are more than thirty thousand promises in the Word of God. Once we begin to understand the nature of these promises and our own potential to see them fulfilled, we will begin to mature in our walk of faith. These promises are designed to activate our confidence in God. Once we realize that He has made abundant personal promises to us, our minds will be enlightened, and we will catch sight of what God is doing in this world. At that point, nothing else will matter. All the things that we have put before the Lordship of Christ will fade into insignificance. Once you taste of the great things that God has for you, you will never want to go back to a mediocre spiritual walk with Him.

Once we catch sight of the promise, we must continually keep the promise in view. One of the truths which is taught in the Old

Testament is that our focus and attention must be on God and not on man. That is why the priests carried the ark into the water first, so the people could see it before them. That is also why the people obediently and confidently followed. As we keep the promises of God continually before us, we will be motivated to activate those promises in our lives.

Personal worth and value are not things which can merely be attributed to our income, possessions, or status in life. In the ultimate sense, our own personal worth can only be determined in light of the death of Christ for us. If God were willing to do that for us, then how much more can we trust Him with every detail of our lives? Just as the Israelites focused straight ahead on the ark of the covenant as the waters of the Jordan divided, so must we do the same. When the storms of life billow against you, keep your eyes on the Promiser and not the circumstances. Remember, being a Christian will not make you immune to the problems of life. But the exciting news for believers is that God's promises are greater than our problems.

When the problems become the toughest, God's promises become the dearest. It is only in light of the great tragedies and necessities of life that we really begin to fully understand and appreciate the depth and significance of God's promises to us. As we begin to claim those promises and see them beautifully fulfilled in our lives, we understand that God is the One who alone can bring us through the difficulties and set us on solid ground.

Make Promises Become Reality

In the Book of Joshua, chapter 3, the Bible presents three prerequisites for seeing God's promises come to pass.

A Clean Heart

As Joshua prepared the children of Israel for their miraculous crossing, he told them to "sanctify yourselves" (v. 5). He was calling upon them to repent and cleanse their hearts so that they might serve the Lord. There are many promises of God recorded in Scripture which will never be fulfilled in our lives if we merely attempt to claim them in the arm of the flesh. We cannot expect God to move miraculously on our behalf to fulfill His promises to us unless our hearts are right with Him.

Spiritual heart surgery takes diligence and discipline. It involves cutting away that which is displeasing to God and replacing it with that which pleases Him. In many ways the Christian life involves the same kind of diligence and precise care as medical heart surgery. Only when our hearts are right with God can we expect the fulfillment of His promises in our lives.

A Focused Mind

Not only were the Israelites to properly prepare themselves spiritually by the means of spiritual sanctification, but they were also to focus their attention on the ark of the covenant, and thereby, on God Himself. Leaving behind their negative traditions, they focused on the future. When Joshua told the people of Israel to follow the priests into the Jordan River, they could have easily questioned the wisdom of such a command. But, by this time, the Israelites had learned that obedience was certainly a better option than disobedience. When the priests stepped forward, the people readily followed after them.

Most of us have difficulty attempting great things for God because we are so unwilling to break with tradition. If it hasn't been done before, we are reluctant to be the first ones to take a step of faith in a new direction. Although some traditions can be healthy and need to be followed, others can destroy vision and cause us to come up on the short end of what God has for us.

I remember hearing the story of a man who walked into the kitchen one day when his wife was preparing to bake a ham. He had noticed it was always her tradition to cut off the end of the ham before she baked it. He had wondered why she did it that way, so he asked her. "Honey," he said, "why do you always cut off the end of the ham before you cook it?" "I don't know," she replied, "It's just the way my mother always did it." *Now,* he thought to himself, *when her mother comes for Thanksgiving, I'll ask her why it's done that way.* When Thanksgiving came, the man asked his mother-in-law, "Mother, why do you always cut off the end of the ham before you cook it?" "Oh," she said, "I really don't know for sure, it's just the way my mother taught me to do it." Now he was really exasperated! *Well,* he thought, *when Grandmother comes for Christmas, I'll ask her why she does it that way.* So Christmas finally came and the man asked his grandmother-in-law, "Grandmother, when you cook hams, why do you always cut off the ends before you cook them?" "Oh, son," she replied, "I always cut off the ends because I have a short pan!"

I never hear that story without thinking about the joys that have been missed, the gifts of God that we have all been robbed of, and the many who could have been, but were not, won to Christ, because so many Christians have bound themselves to the traditions of others who had spiritually short pans. Whatever you attempt to do for God, keep your eyes focused upon Him and get a big pan!

What the Israelites had come to understand under Joshua's leadership was that God was a big God and able to fulfill His promises then and there. Remember, these were not the Israelites who had crossed the Red Sea, for most of them had died in the wilderness. This was a younger generation who had been born in that wilderness experience and heard the stories their parents had told them of God's miraculous deliverance forty years earlier.

It is our tendency today to concentrate on the stories of spiritual revival and awakening in the past. We often hear accounts of the great moving of God in the days of Whitfield, Wesley, and Edwards. Or we hear about the revivals of Finney, Moody, and Sunday. But rarely do we talk about what God is doing today! The truth is that the same miracle-working power that was available to believers in generations gone by is available to us today. We, too, can expect by faith to see God at work on our behalf when our hearts are right and our minds are focused on Him.

Unquestioned Obedience

Joshua told the priests to put the ark of the covenant upon their shoulders and to step into the waters of the Jordan River. Then he told the people to follow them across the river to the other side. The Israelites did not stand there and argue with Joshua or try to present an alternative plan. They had no minority report to deliver and no votes to take. They moved ahead with unquestioned obedience.

Unfortunately, we rarely see that kind of obedience demonstrated in God's people today. We tend to obey only when we are virtually forced to, and even then it is usually without the right heart attitude. Too often we are like the little boy who was standing on the chair at the dinner table. When his mother insisted that he sit down, he refused to do so. Therefore, she spanked him and made him sit in the chair. As he was sitting there, she remarked, "Now, don't you feel better sitting down?"

"No!" he insisted. "I'm still standing on the inside!"

Such half-hearted obedience will never bring the blessing of God upon your life. If you really want to see the promises of God fulfilled in your life, surrender to Him in unquestioned obedience and you will experience His unlimited power.

Expect the Miracle!

There is one other factor which is necessary in order to see God's promises fulfilled for us: We must *expect* those promises to be fulfilled. That is where the elements of faith and confidence enter in. It is one thing to know what God's promises are, and to even believe that they could be fulfilled; but it is another thing to *expect* them to be fulfilled. It is at this point that we actualize our faith. Believers often take the attitude that God might fulfill His promises to others, but not to them. We can even become excited when someone else has an answered prayer, but we rarely expect such answers to our own personal needs. True faith believes God's promises and trusts Him for their fulfillment.

If Joshua and the people of Israel had not expected God to fulfill His word, they would have turned back into the wilderness, even as their forefathers did. Instead, they realized that they were in a position to trust God as they never had before and put Him to the test. And it was a difficult position, to say the least: crossing the swollen River Jordan with hostile enemy forces waiting for them on the other side. Yet, it was exactly where they needed to be—where they were absolutely forced to expect God to deliver them. It is in such moments of faith that God is pleased to bless us and show His faithfulness in our deliverance.

You may not have such rivers to cross in your own life today. But one day you'll find yourself, as we all do, in some situation in which only God can help you. When that day comes, remember that the God who delivered the people of Israel can deliver you as well. His help, love, and power are just as real today as ever. Trust Him, claim His promises, and you will not be disappointed.

Here, then, is a wonderful formula for seeing the fulfillment of God's promises. Put it to the test. I think you will find it greatly rewarding.

HOW TO HAVE GOD'S PROMISES FULFILLED
God's Word on the Matter + A Clean Heart + A Focused Mind
+ Unquestioned Obedience = Promises Fulfilled

"But I'm afraid to take that first step," you say. Fear is common to human nature. We are all afraid of something at some time in our lives. But God can give you the courage to overcome your fears—the courage to face the future and make it your own.

Take Advantage of the Moment

Courage is something which most of us lack—especially in the face of opposition. It is easy to talk about having courage, but it is another matter altogether to have it at the moment we need it. Sometimes we lack the courage to admit our weaknesses and call out for help. I can recall as a child being afraid in the dark, and yet also being too afraid to call out to anyone to help me. At other times we lack the courage to take hold of some once-in-a-lifetime opportunity that is set before us, and when the opportunity comes, we sit in silence, and live the rest of our lives wondering why we didn't seize the moment of chance when we had it.

There is a beautiful story told from the life of Christ about a man named Bartimaeus. He was blind and desperately in need of the miracle touch of Christ. The Scripture tells us that as Jesus was leaving Jericho, He was followed by a great crowd of people. Bartimaeus, who was sitting by the roadside begging, heard from the crowd that Jesus of Nazareth was passing by.

Realizing that this moment was his one chance to be healed, Bartimaeus cried out for Jesus to help him. Those surrounding the beggar said, "Bartimaeus, hold your peace—keep quiet and don't bother Jesus." Ignoring them, he cried out all the louder and more fervently for help. Hearing his cry, Jesus stood still and commanded that they bring the blind man to Him. The courage of this poor, blind beggar should challenge our own hearts. At the moment of his greatest need, he was unwilling to sit quietly by and let this opportunity escape him. Instead, he cried out until he attracted Jesus' attention and the Savior stopped and responded.

This account is found in Mark 10:46–52. It is a wonderful illustration of Christ's miracle-working ministry. When our Lord asked the blind man what he wanted, Bartimaeus responded that he desired to receive his sight. Jesus then said, "Go thy way; thy faith hath made thee whole" (v. 52). The Scripture says Bartimaeus *immediately* received his sight and followed after Jesus.

While you may acknowledge that this is a marvelous story, you may also wonder how it applies to your own life. The same principles which were at work in the transformation of Bartimaeus are still at work in our lives today. Perhaps you are struggling with a deep personal problem even at this very moment. You may be so overwhelmed that you are losing the courage to even face life itself! Remember, God's love and miracle-working power are just as available today as they were during the time when our Savior walked upon this earth. What happened to Bartimaeus in that time is no different from what can happen to you today.

God is still in the miracle-working business. All that is needed are the proper ingredients of righteousness and the catalyst of courage to set into motion the power of God for us all.

Acknowledge Your Need

One of the most amazing aspects of the account of Jesus' healing of Bartimaeus is the fact that our Lord responded to his plea by asking him what he wanted. It had to be obvious to Christ that the man was blind and that his request would be related to that particular need. However, Jesus made Bartimaeus express that need personally.

As strange as it sounds, many people never receive the help they need because they lack the courage to admit their need. In the account of Bartimaeus, there were really two miracles: one of physical healing, and one of spiritual healing.

Many people are spiritually blind and do not know it. The great irony of life is that while physical blindness is obvious to everyone, spiritual blindness is not. Many of those who are spiritually blind try to convince themselves that their view of life is adequate and sufficient. But the Bible says that a person is spiritually blind when he has never seen what Jesus Christ can do for him. Second Corinthians 4:4 says, "The god of this world hath blinded the minds of them which believe not." When you cannot see who Christ is and what He has done for you, then Satan has blinded you to the truth of what life is really all about. Satan is the most miserable character in the universe. He is a loser who has already been defeated by the powerful atonement of Christ on the cross.

Have you ever observed a losing ball team? They usually are filled with complaints and excuses. Their heads are hung down and their countenance has fallen in such a way that their misery is obvious to everyone. That is how Satan is! He is a miserable, defeated loser. Unfortunately, in his misery, he is also out to cheat you out of the joy and hope which God has provided for you. He will actually attempt to tell you that the Christian life is the most miserable thing that you could ever experience. If you believe him, you will be blind to the truth of what life is really all about.

I remember hearing a story not long ago about two boys from the country who were riding on a train for the very first time. As they sat in their seats, and looked out of the windows, they were filled with amazement. The train was zooming and the scenery was flashing past their eyes as they gazed in wonder. Eventually a porter came through the car selling bananas. Each boy bought one, and about the time the first boy took a bite of his banana, the train went into a deep, dark, long tunnel. As the two boys sat in stunned silence, one said to the other, "John, have you eaten your banana yet?" "No, why?" his friend responded. "Well, don't do it, cause if you do, it'll make you blind as a bat!"

We can laugh at this ridiculous story, but the lies of the devil make just as little sense. He wants to blind us to the real cause-and-effect relationships of life. He is especially delighted when we are blind to God's power which is available to us and His provisions to meet our needs. Remember, the first step in finding the miracle you need is to have the courage to acknowledge your need in the first place.

Ask God for Help

When Bartimaeus heard that Jesus was passing by, he immediately began to cry out. He did not merely sit there and consider his options. He did something about it! He cried out as loudly as he could, in spite of the throng of people around him. While the beggar's shouts may have been an embarrassment to his friends, desperate people know no embarrassment. Bartimaeus not only cried out persistently, but he also called out, "Jesus, thou Son of David." Such a reference was an acknowledgment of the claim of Jesus to be the Messiah, the descendant of David. Thus, Bartimaeus's appeal was directly made to the authority of Christ Himself. It was that request which stopped our Lord in His tracks.

You may be facing a crisis in your own life at this very moment. If you are, do not hesitate to call upon God for help. In the face of our greatest calamities, God's great grace can overcome any obstacle that we face. In such times of need, we must learn to pray with a sincerity and fervency that reaches from the very depth of our being. When you become desperate enough to seek God with all your heart, realizing that He is the only solution to your problems, then you will receive courage to trust God for a miracle in your behalf.

Be Ready to Respond

The Scripture tells us that Bartimaeus cast away his garment, rose, and came to Jesus. Notice that Christ did not come to the beggar, but rather that He called the beggar to come to Him. Virtually every miracle that God does on our behalf demands a response from us personally.

Bartimaeus had probably been sitting by the wayside of that dusty road for years. His garment was undoubtedly filthy, and the beggar himself was anything but an example of cleanliness. At the same time, that garment was all the security that Bartimaeus had with which to clothe himself. But in this moment of greatest possibility, he was willing to throw it aside, parting with his false and unclean garment of security in order to come into the presence of the Lord.

Why is it people think they can come to God clutching the rags of their own sinful lifestyles and expect God to work in their behalf?

If there is one great theme of the Bible it is that God is holy. He is separated from sin and can have no fellowship with it. The first step toward coming to God is confessing our sins, casting off the filthy garments of transgressions, and then approaching His throne of grace. He will receive us in no other way: only after we have, through His forgiveness, cleaned up our hearts.

Louis XIV of France was one of the greatest kings who ever lived. He was also apparently one of the filthiest men who ever lived. It is said that he only took a bath once a year, and that he only did that because his doctors insisted upon it. They literally held him down and bathed him annually. In fact, he was so unwilling to bathe on a regular basis that he eventually commissioned a chemist to develop a substance that he could put on his body so that he would never have to take another bath. The chemist eventually developed that substance from the pollen of flowers and presented it to the king. Every morning Louis XIV doused himself with this liquid so that people could stand to be in his presence. That substance was known as perfume.

We can douse ourselves with the perfume of good works and noble efforts for an entire lifetime and never experience the cleansing grace of God. We can attend church, give money to the Sunday School, and even tell others about Jesus Christ without ever coming to personal faith in Him ourselves.

The Bible never teaches us that God's acceptance is dependent upon our good works. If we had to cleanse ourselves from sin, we would all perish. However, the Bible does tell us that God has made cleansing possible to all who will come to Him by faith. The prophet Isaiah said, "Come now, let us reason together, saith the LORD: though your sins be as scarlet, they shall be as white as snow; though they be red like crimson, they shall be as wool" (Isa. 1:18). The psalmist said, "As far as the east is from the west, so far hath he removed our transgressions from us" (Ps. 103:12). The apostle Peter said, "Repent ye therefore, and be converted, that your sins may be blotted out" (Acts 3:19). The apostle John put it this way, "If we confess our sins, he is faithful and just to forgive us our sins, and to cleanse us from all unrighteousness" (1 John 1:9).

What greater promises could anyone have? God has clearly stated in His Word that He will make every provision to cleanse us from our sins, blot them out, remove them, wash them, and forgive them. There is nothing that we can do to save ourselves; He has done it all. In light of that, the only response we need to make is to cast ourselves upon His grace and to trust His wonderful provision as adequate payment for our sins, believing the promise of His invitation is for us personally. It is no wonder that the hymn writer said,

What can wash away my sins?
Nothing but the blood of Jesus.

Accept God's Offer

There must also come a point in our lives when we must have the courage to accept God's provision for our needs. Had Bartimaeus remained silent, there would not have been any solution to the problem of his blindness. But, in his moment of opportunity, he received the miracle of courage to cry out by faith for that which only Christ could do for him. Shouting above the din of the crowd, Bartimaeus caught the attention of the Savior, and Jesus called him to come to Him. When Bartimaeus requested the restoration of his sight, Jesus simply said, "Go thy way; thy faith hath made thee whole" (Mark 10:52). The Bible tells us that the beggar immediately "received his sight, and followed Jesus in the way." This literally means that he became a follower of Jesus Christ. The term *the way* was the early phrase by which Christianity was known. The concept comes from the Old Testament term *hallachah* which means "a way of life." In other words, Jesus Christ became the way of life for Bartimaeus. Hence, Jesus' early disciples were known as followers of "the way."

From that day on, Bartimaeus was known to one and all as the man whom Jesus healed. He would be known as one who walked with Christ Himself. Just as He passed by Bartimaeus so many years ago, Christ is passing your way today. Take advantage of the moment and call out to Him from the depth of your need. Just as He met the need of that blind beggar, He will meet your needs as well.

I have a plaque that someone gave me several years ago. Under the title "COURAGE" are these words by an unnamed writer who understood the true definition of courage.

Why is it that most men's lives are controlled by small and petty circumstances? I am saddened as I watch people lose the good and great things that are within their reach and could be theirs with "but a little act of courage!"

Courage is the most beautiful of all human expressions. Courage as I see it is, "an act in the face of fear." We only need courage when we are afraid, which means that we need courage almost all of the time, because we are afraid of something all of the time.

I have discovered that fear becomes a coward when faced with but a small act of courage, and further, that the muscle of courage will grow strong with continued use.

My advice to myself is, "do those things which you fear, and keep doing them until you are no longer afraid, and then you will have become the master of your fate."

I have studied the deeds of men both great and small, and I have studied those men who are great and small. In this study there appear to be many differences. All of the differences which count have, at their base, one single thing—courage.

Courage is that one ingredient which separates the weak from the strong, the successful from the weak, the great from the average. All the things you desire in life have one common handle, which is made for the hand of the person with courage. To be afraid is to be alive. To act in the face of fear is to be a man.

Focus on the Future

1. What promises are you claiming from God for your future?

_____

_____

2. What obstacles are you facing in making those promises become a reality?

_____

_____

3. What steps of action do you need to take to overcome these obstacles?

   _____

   _____

   _____

4. Focus on this thought: God is the author of all my tomorrows. He can provide all I need to make my future bright.

3

Living Stable in an Unstable World

In his national bestseller *Seven Habits of Highly Effective People,* Stephen Covey explains that life is made up of the things which we believe. He calls these paradigms. Covey writes, "Paradigms are powerful because they create the lenses through which we see the world."[1] They are patterns of beliefs which, like colored lenses, determine the way we see reality. Doug Murren, in *Leadershift,* adds, "When several people, such as a church, share these paradigms, they have common views of reality."[2]

One of the basic principles of psychology is that of perception. We tend to believe what we perceive to be true. Now there are some things that we believe are absolutely true. These truths are expressed in inspired Scripture. However, there are many perceptions that we hold in life which are only true to our particular viewpoint. Having lived most of my life in the South, my perception of the War Between the States may be quite different from someone's perception who lived most of his life in the North. As a Baptist pastor, my perception of local church ministry may be quite different from that of a Lutheran pastor. Even within our own congregations, there exist different perceptions of reality.

One of the basic principles of psychology is that of perception. We tend to believe what we perceive to be true.

In most churches, majority perceptions prevail. The concept of what makes for a successful church, or even a successful service, is the result of a collective mindset held by the majority of the people in the church. It is this collective mentality which sets the boundaries and parameters of the ministry of the church. In order to change the direction of ministry, one must change those perceptions. For example, years ago the idea of using a live band or orchestra in a Sunday morning service was considered beyond the boundaries of acceptable church worship. However, those same congregations were willing to tolerate, and even enjoy, the use of musical sound tracks which actually included all of those very same instruments. The difference was that the audience heard the music, but they never saw the drums, guitars, and percussion instruments. As churches became more accepting of musical sound tracks, they became more accepting of a live band or orchestra.

Why are paradigms so important? Because they define our present existence and determine how we will face the future. As times change, our patterns of worship and styles of ministry change. Our paradigms must change as well. Unless people become convinced that doing ministry differently is biblically sound and correct, they will resist it. I can recall a time when singles ministries that were focused on the needs of divorced singles were beyond the parameter of the average church's way of thinking. Some even objected that such a ministry would in itself encourage divorce. But over a period of time, it has become evident that singles ministries are not only needed, but are effective in helping those who have been victimized by divorce, and who are looking to the church for help in solving their personal problems. Most larger churches today would not think of attempting to minister in a society where there is a 50 percent divorce rate without a full-time singles minister.

Years ago, counseling ministries were virtually unheard of in a church. What little counseling was done was performed by the pastor in private sessions. The idea of small groups formed around spiritual and psychological support for dealing with some of the difficulties of life was beyond the parameters of the paradigm of most churches. Today, it is quite common for churches to employ full-time counselors, often providing office space for a professional outsider to counsel with church members.

All of these changes involve paradigm shifts in the way people thought about the church and its ministry. Doug Murren provides this list of the significance of paradigms:

1. Paradigms lay out a pattern of life and give us boundaries within which to define success.
2. Paradigms provide a lens through which we observe reality.
3. Paradigms establish the rules and definitions of the game we are playing, and get us all on the same page.
4. Paradigms give structure and meaning to our actions.
5. Paradigms allow us to move ahead into the future with a common focus as a group.[3]

Those who are willing to face the challenges of the future and lead people into that future must have the ability to see the future in light of the will and purpose of God. Those who are willing to take the risks of new structures of ministry must also be willing to shift long-established paradigms in order to accomplish their goals. Such leaders have the ability to envision new things and to perceive a bright future. It's true you cannot prevent change, but you can channel it!

It's All in Your Mind

Real change begins on the inside before it takes effect on the outside. Merely changing the externals of life is like rearranging the furniture in your office without redirecting your goals, patterns, or leadership

> *Real change begins on the inside before it takes effect on the outside.*

styles. The most effective change always begins within the heart and mind of the individual.

Spiritual hope comes from the Holy Spirit within us. As He dwells in our hearts, He enables us to see the external world from God's point of view. The Spirit helps us see our present struggle in view of eternal realities. This alone is what enables us to live by faith, because this faith focuses on the mind, heart, and character of God.

The indwelling Holy Spirit produces the reality of spiritual life within us. God never tells us how to live and then expects us to do it on our own. He lives through us so that we can experience the abundant life He has planned for us. You can live *above* life's difficulties, problems, and pressures. Because God lives in us, He makes all the difference!

Psychiatrist Larry Crabb observes this process in his classic work *Inside Out*. In his book, Dr. Crabb expresses his basic theory of human behavior. All true change must begin *inside* before it changes us *outside*.

Dr. Crabb raises his reader's hope for a better life by reminding them that mere effort isn't the answer. "Looking for more hoops to jump through," is not the way to follow God according to Dr. Crabb. Moreover, he asserts finding God's peace "requires an honest look into your life." Jumping through hoops may be easier than facing what is really inside, he observes, but he concludes: "An inside look can lead to real change. Change from the inside out."[4]

The greatest inhibitor to spiritual development is self-reliance. The more we are convinced that we can handle the pressures of life ourselves, the less likely we are to turn to the One who alone can really help us.

In his discussion of this, Dr. Crabb comes to the conclusion that real life only comes to fruition with the death of self-reliance. He writes, "Because our soul is so thoroughly stained with self-reliance, the death of pride feels like the death of our self. However, the more terrible the blow to our efforts to preserve our own life, or minimize our pain, the more we are merged as truly alive. The process seems confusing only because it cuts across our ideas about how to live."[5]

The real paradigm shifts must occur within our own hearts. When we are forced to take an honest look at ourselves, we are more likely to discover what we are all about in the first place. In order to make the kind of changes that will equip us to deal with the issues of the future, we must begin by dealing with our own resistance to change.

At every juncture in church history, the struggle of shifting paradigms has always become the major conflict within the church. The early church struggled with what to do with so many Gentile converts. The Medieval Church struggled with the shift away from Latin. They had elevated Latin to the status of a sacred language. To give up Latin became a paradigm comparable to giving up God! During the time of the Great Revivals, prayer meetings became a symbol of spirituality. Hence, midweek service was added to the church schedule.

What is true on the church level is also true on the personal level. Our personal commitment to seek the Lord in prayer, to study the Scripture, or to actively engage in a task in evangelism all grow out of our own particular views of Christian spirituality. We do what we do because we believe what we believe. Our beliefs trigger our behavior. We become what we think.

> *At every juncture in church history, the struggle of shifting paradigms has always become the major conflict within the church.*

Jesus explained this process of internal change when He said, "There is nothing from without a man, that entering into him can defile him: but the things which come out of him, those are they that defile the man" (Mark 7:15). When the disciples asked the Lord to explain this process, He told them that life is more than the externals that make it up. Real life begins within the depths and souls of men. Our Lord added, "For from within, out of the heart of men, proceed evil thoughts . . . all these evil things come from within, and defile the man" (Mark 7:20–23).

Spiritual conflict occurs within us. By the same token, spiritual change must begin within us as well. Mike Flynn and Doug Gregg discuss this in their helpful book *Inner Healing.*[6] They point out that sin harms our inner being to such a degree that it can only be corrected through the process of repentance that results in the healing of our emotions. What Flynn and Gregg are trying to help us understand is that real lasting change must begin within the hearts of individuals. They simplify this process in three basic steps:

1. We listen.
2. God speaks.
3. We obey.

We can read the Scripture but not be moved by its truths. We can pray and say words but fail to communicate with God. We can attend church and go through the motions of worship, but never really worship the true and living God. Ed Young calls this "flat land living."[7] The old-timers called it "spiritual declension." In the nineteenth century, Octavius Winslow defined it like this: "A secret decay of the health, vigour and exercise of grace in the soul."[8]

When the heart stops ascending toward God, it begins descending away from Him. My father used to say, "When you stop growing, you start dying." To which I would add, "Whatever is happening on the inside eventually shows up on the outside!"

Why Do We Do the Things We Do?

Have you ever asked yourself why you do what you do? Perhaps you have come under conviction about some habit or practice in your life and determined not to do it again. The Holy Spirit seemed to convict your heart and challenged you to change your lifestyle.

"All right, God," you said, "I admit what I've done is wrong, and I promise I won't do it again."

With new determination you faced Monday morning with a real sense of victory. You made it through Tuesday, Wednesday, and Thursday. But by Friday, you found yourself falling flat on your face again. Frustrated and discouraged, you may have asked yourself, "Why am I like this?"

Such a struggle is not unique. The apostle Paul himself described his own struggle with the internal forces of his life (see Rom. 7:19–25). He reminds us that to win the war between the spirit and the flesh, we need to understand the nature of the conflict. It is a spiritual struggle, raging within us. The external actions of our lives are merely a reflection of that internal conflict.

The Nature of the Flesh

The sin nature we were all born with is a fleshly nature. It cries out for the gratification of the flesh. Even our best deeds cannot eradicate that sinful nature. We can attend church, give money to the poor, sing in the choir, and go through all the motions of religion— still we are nothing more than filthy rags! It is no wonder that the prophet Jeremiah said, "The heart is deceitful above all things, and desperately wicked: who can know it?" (Jer. 17:9).

The Nature of the Spirit

The Bible reminds us that God's solution to our problem is the provision of a "new heart" or a "new birth." When it occurs, a marvelous thing happens within us. We receive a new nature which is born in us by the power of the Holy Spirit. Theologians call this process *regeneration*. It means being reborn—born by the power of the Holy Spirit. When it occurs, we become alive spiritually for the first time in our lives. Before that, we were just going through the motions of human existence. But once we are born of the Spirit, we begin to live!

The Nature of the Conflict

Spiritual conversion results from regeneration by the Holy Spirit. But it doesn't eradicate the fleshly nature within us. That fleshly (carnal) nature is our spiritual battleground. Therefore, it is inevitable there will be a spiritual conflict within each one of us.

The apostle Paul describes this inner struggle in Galatians 5:17, where he writes, "The flesh lusteth against the Spirit, and the Spirit against the flesh." He further describes these two natures as "contrary the one to the other." We often find ourselves being tempted to do the very things we really don't want to do.

Life becomes a series of choices. From the time you get up in the morning until you go to bed at night, your life is filled with choices. Whatever choices you make will determine the outcome of your life. Practically, this means letting the Spirit within you determine your outward actions. Ultimately, it means choosing between the Spirit and the flesh.

Let's make this practical and apply it to the issue of facing the future. Some of us are afraid of the future. When we look at the external threats and pressures of life, we want to run into the safety of our own little predictable paradigm. It is difficult for us to risk stepping over the boundaries of lifelong patterns in order to lead the way to the future. But this is exactly what each one of us must continue to do.

Steve helped in our church youth ministry. At a key point in his life, he really struggled with giving up his job, his friends, and his security in order to take a step of faith regarding full-time Christian work. As we talked about his struggle and his decision, he commented, "I understand there's a struggle going on with me. But what can I do about it? How can I win this battle?" Here's what I told him:

Recognize that the future is in the hand of God. The future is not just what you make it to be. It is the inevitable result of the sovereign will and purpose of God for your life. Your ability to face the future, with all of its challenges, and to successfully negotiate the changes that are necessary to deal with the future, depend upon your willingness to let God be in control of your life.

Realize the consequences of failure. If we do not shift our thought paradigms, and adjust our actions accordingly, we will remain the prisoners of the past. We will never be properly prepared to face the future and take full advantage of the opportunities made to us. Remember, every generation of Christians has had to face an uncertain future. All one has to do is read the classics of church history to understand that this is true. You are not alone in your struggle. Other generations have faced the same pressures and had to make the same adjustments.

Rely on God to guide you. The Scripture reminds us, "Greater is he that is in you, than he that is in the world" (1 John 4:4). Spiritual warfare is a normal past of the Christian life. But the promise of God is that He will empower us to overcome the world by the power of His Spirit. If you want to win the battle within, rely on the Holy Spirit for the ultimate triumph in your life.

God Will Change You Outwardly

The apostle Paul is the prime example of the changing power of God. Prior to his conversion to Christ, Paul was centered upon himself.

He studied diligently, glorified his knowledge, and sought to elevate himself through his adherence to Jewish law. Paul went about persecuting Christians, slaying them and dragging them off to jail. All of this was intended to enable him to work his way up in the political structure of ancient Judaism. It was all for self! But once he met Jesus Christ, his eyes turned from self to the cross, then to others.

Jesus changes our focus. When a person really has an encounter with Christ, his focus is changed from one who elevates himself to one who cares about others. He changes from a person who says, "What can you do for me?" to a person who says, "What can I do for you?"

A survey done by national advertisers found that the most important question on the minds of the American public is, "What's in it for me?" While this may be the typical American mindset, it's not the mindset of God! He wants what is best for us by teaching us to want what's best for others!

God Will Change You Inwardly

Real change affects the inner person. It changes one's motivation, values, and beliefs. In the earlier part of the twentieth century, a phrenologist—one who studies the skull—came to Gypsy Smith, a great evangelist, and asked a favor.

"Gypsy, I want to feel your skull and find out the secret of your success," he said.

Gypsy replied, "Sir, if you're going to find out the secret of my success, you need to feel my heart!"

The God who changes the heart changes the inner life of the man. When we are changed on the inside, the results of

> *Real change affects the inner person. It changes one's motivation, values, and beliefs.*

that change then flow on the outside. People begin to see the evidence of a work of God within, by observing our behavior without. When that kind of change occurs, we begin to see the world as God sees it. Instead of taking a negative view about the challenges of the future, we begin to see the future from God's point of view. That results in the development of true wisdom. Hope springs from *within*. Living by faith is living by confidence in the will of God. It means trusting the very nature and character of God Himself.

The person who knows his future is in the hands of God can anticipate that future in hope and confidence. He is not ultimately affected by social and political change. He is not defeated by external setbacks. Rather, he rises above the circumstances of life because the God who is above the circumstances lives within him.

The Holy Spirit produces within us the very qualities we need to face the pressures of life. Galatians 5:22–23 describes these as the *fruit of the Spirit:*

love	goodness
joy	faith
peace	meekness
patience	self-control

When these qualities are produced in us, they enable us to deal with the external realities of life. The Bible never encourages us to tackle the pressures of life by our own efforts. Rather, the Scripture reminds us of our need for total dependence upon God. He is the only one who can do *in* you that which will change you, so that *out* of you will flow the evidence of that internal change.

Changed! Inside out. That is how real change has always worked. The only way you'll ever be prepared to face the demands of the future is by allowing God to change you from within.

In his powerful book *The Man in the Mirror,* Patrick Morley observes: "The Christian pilgrimage is a moment-by-moment, daily journey. It requires daily effort, without which we will stray. . . . Few lives are stagnant and unchanging. Usually our spiritual lives march forward or they slip backwards. Life is like the treadmill in your doctor's office. If you stop walking forward, you lose ground. . . . The pen is in your hands now, so go ahead . . . write the next chapter!"[9]

The unlimited power of God is a reservoir within you. Let Him open the floodgates and release His power!

Focus on the Future

1. Reflect for a moment on how you perceive the world around you. Is it hostile? Friendly? Neutral? Stable? Changing? Challenging? Boring?

2. Make a list of the basic beliefs that make up your personal paradigm:

Family _____

Religion _____

Values _____

Beliefs _____

Work_____

3. What changes are occurring *inside* your life these days? How are they being expressed externally?

_____

_____

_____

4

Your Dreams Can Come True

I think we all want to count in life. We want to make a difference some how, some way, in our world.

The little girl shuts herself in her room and dances with dreams of one day being a ballerina. The freckled-faced boy bounces the ball off the side of the house, catching it in his glove and dreaming of the Big Leagues. The student dreams of a diploma; the graduate, that promising new job; the worker, that long-sought-after promotion.

What do all these people have in common? They are dreaming that they will count for something—that one day they will "make it in life." They are dreaming that because of them, things will be different.

I have good news for everyone who has dreamed such dreams: God created every one to make a difference in this world. There is no one who doesn't count. Everyone is an essential part of His plan.

In his book *Power Thoughts,* Robert Schuller makes this insightful observation:

> God knew what he was doing when he established the "belief" system. Strip away all mystery, leave all truth naked and mathematically and scientifically exposed, and something sweet and romantic will be removed.
>
> Twinkle, twinkle little star,
> I know exactly what you are:

41

An incandescent ball of gas,
Condensing to a solid mass!

There must always be the unknown. There must always be
the unprovable. For faith confronts these frontiers with a
thrilling leap and life becomes vibrant with adventure.
Faith is dreaming God's dream.[1]

It is our ability to dream that makes us unique. We have been
created in the image of God. Therefore, we can dream, hope, and plan.
These are the expressions of His will in our lives.

Dreaming is:

• what you want to be;
• where you want to go;
• what you want to do;
• goals you'd like to reach;
• plans you'd like to make;
• projects you hope to achieve.

Faith is the key that places your dreams and aspirations into the
hands of God. He is able to cause all our dreams to come true and
reach their fullest potential.

There is no greater story in the Bible to illustrate this than the
miracle found in John 6:5–14. Jesus and His disciples were faced
with a challenging situation. As Christ had begun teaching upon a
mountainside, a great multitude had gathered to hear Him. The
Bible says there were about five thousand
men in the crowd that day. When these
people became hungry, the disciples were
perplexed at how they would feed them
all. What would they do?

> *It is our ability to dream that makes us unique. We have been created in the image of God. Therefore, we can dream, hope, and plan.*

At that very moment, Andrew, one of
the disciples, announced there was a small
boy in the crowd who had five barley
loaves and two fish, adding, "But what are
they among so many?" (v.9).

The Lord took the food which the boy
had surrendered to Him, blessed the loaves, and gave them to the disciples to distribute to the people. Then Jesus did the same thing with
the fish. As the disciples moved from person to person handing out

bread, there continued to be an endless supply left in their hands, and likewise with the fish. In fact, the Bible tells us that when they were finished, they had not only fed the entire multitude but they also collected twelve baskets full of leftover fragments!

Imagine, one small boy, through a simple act of surrender, became the central figure in one of the most phenomenal miracles that Jesus ever performed. His sacrifice made a difference for thousands of people. In the same way, you and I can never underestimate the significance of a single act of surrender on our part in our own day and age; we, too, can be part of God's miracle in our world.

Perhaps you are just living from day to day. Perhaps there doesn't seem to be any special significance about your life at all. You simply get up in the morning, go to work for the day, and go to bed at night. Your life is caught in the routines of life and doesn't seem to have any real purpose. Perhaps you feel a little like the man in the following poem:

> Poor, poor, Solomon Grundy,
> Born on Monday,
> Christened on Tuesday,
> Married on Wednesday,
> Sick on Thursday,
> Sicker on Friday,
> Died on Saturday,
> Buried on Sunday,
> And that was the end of Solomon Grundy.

It may be that in the daily grind you feel that life isn't worth living after all. You have once dreamed great dreams, but now you feel your dreams have died. Well, if that is the case, I've good news for you. You can dream again! You can see your dreams come true as you learn the secret of surrendering your life to the God who makes dreams come true. In the story of this one little boy who was a vital part of Jesus' miracle, we find principles that can make dreams happen.

The Right Place at the Right Time

Notice that the little boy was in the right place at the right time. Just when the disciples were most desperate to decide what to do about the needs of the multitude, this boy appeared with his lunch. We are not told who he was, where he came from, or how he got there. He may well have come with his parents, or perhaps he had left home that morning with a lunch packed by a thoughtful mother and had made his way to the edge of town to hear this wonderful Teacher. Whatever the case may have been, the boy was in exactly the right place to offer his simple act of surrender which touched the lives of thousands of people that day.

Finding success in the will of God also depends upon being in the right place at the right time. I have often heard people in business comment on the success of someone else by saying, "Oh, he was just lucky to be in the right place at the right time." But I have found that, more often than not, successful people are in the right place at the right time because they have already made certain important decisions that placed them there.

> *Finding success in the will of God also depends upon being in the right place at the right time.*

For example, the little boy we just read about was in the right place at the right time because someone, either he or his mother, had taken time to prepare his lunch. Proper preparation will always pay off. This is true in every area of our lives. In business or vocation, we may eventually benefit from years of preparation, organization, and planning. In other instances, a limited amount of preparation may bring immediate benefits. Whatever the case may be, the point is that things just don't happen by accident.

In the Christian life, there are specific things that we can know for certain. First of all, I can be sure that I am in a right relationship with God. The Bible tells us that Jesus Christ died for our sins so that He might reconcile us to God. It is possible for each of us to know beyond a shadow of a doubt that our sins have been forgiven and that our lives have been committed to Christ.

Second, we can also know for certain that we are in the center of God's will when we are doing the things that He commands us to do. As much as some people struggle to find the will of God for their life, I have always been convinced that the will of God is not hard to find. God has written a manual for us which explains the steps to knowing His will and following it in every detail of our lives. That manual is the Bible. In it, God reveals His plan and purpose for our lives.

In Bible times, the concept of a "will" was similar to what we would call a last will and testament today. It was a specific statement of one's intended purposes, especially between a father and a son. The will of the father stated his relationship to his son as his heir and explained all that the father intended to give to his son. In the same way, the Bible is the specific statement of God's will and testament for the believer.

My son, Jason, now stands over 6'3", and although in my heart he still is my little boy, in reality he is now a young man. Suppose I were to say to him, "Jason, there is something that I want you to do for me. In fact, if you don't do it, you are going to get in trouble. But if you are willing to do it, I'm going to give you a great reward."

Let's assume that he indicates that he is willing to do what I ask. Then, after I remind him that his response will either bring him great joy or great trouble, he asks, "Dad, what is it you want me to do?"

I respond, "I am not going to tell you! I am simply going to let you guess what I want you to do."

Obviously, this is an utterly foolish scenario. No father would rightfully ask his son to do something without explaining what it was he wanted him to do. In fact, if the father were convinced that this would benefit his son, he would tell him very clearly and explicitly what to do. He might even write it down for him so he would not forget it. That is exactly what our heavenly Father has done for us. He has taken the time to write His will for us in black and white in the pages of Scripture.

Discovering God's Will

Let me share with you six ways that I have found to be effective in discovering God's will in my own life. These have aided me in being in the right place at the right time. God's will is revealed in:

Word of God. The psalmist said, "Thy word is a lamp unto my feet, and a light unto my path" (Ps. 119:105). God has detailed His plan in the Bible. To ignore it is to disregard the greatest source of knowing God's will, but to study it carefully and follow it completely is the wisest thing we can do.

Witness of the Holy Spirit. Jesus promised us, "Howbeit when he, the Spirit of truth, is come, he will guide you into all truth: for he shall not speak of himself; but whatsoever he shall hear, that shall he speak: and he will show you things to come" (John 16:13). God has placed within all of His children the presence of the Holy Spirit to guide us. But we must give Him a chance to speak to our hearts through prayer and meditation upon His Word.

Walk of Fellowship. This is the knowledge that comes from our daily walk with God. In the Old Testament we are told that "Enoch walked with God" (Gen. 5:22). We, too, can walk with God each day. The longer we walk with Him in fellowship, the greater our ability to understand His perfect will.

A few months ago, as I was preparing for the funeral service of one of the men in our church, I met with the man's widow and children and asked if they knew of any particular thing that he might like to have done at his funeral. Instantly his wife replied with a certain request. "I know he would have wanted it," she said. One of the daughters looked at her and asked how she could be so certain her father would have wanted it that way. The mother replied, "Honey, I lived with your father for forty-eight years. After that long, I think I would know what he wanted."

The same applies to our walk of fellowship with God. The longer we walk with Him in sweet and close fellowship, the more apt we are to understand His will when we face life's decisions.

Wisdom of God. The apostle James tells us that God will give wisdom liberally to those who ask for it in prayer (see James 1:5). It is reassuring to know that God is ready to give us wisdom if we are willing to ask for it and put ourselves in the relationship with Him in which we can receive it.

Workers of God. These are our fellow believers who have been through many of the trials and tribulations that face us and are willing to give us godly counsel concerning direction for our lives. Remember that "in the multitude of counselors there is safety" (Prov. 11:14).

Works of God. There is a beautiful promise in Psalm 32:8. It says, "I will instruct thee and teach thee in the way which thou shalt go: I

will guide thee with mine eye." Part of
God's guiding process is the opening and
closing of doors of opportunity before us.
This is often the clearest way of discerning
His will.

When God closes a door, we must be careful not to ignore His will by trying to force our way in.

When God closes a door, we must be
careful not to ignore His will by trying to
force our way in. As a man many years my
senior once told me, "Son, if you've prayed about a matter and God
has shut the door, don't go around back and try to crawl through the
window!"

Never forget that God is a loving heavenly Father. All of the gen-
erosity and kindness that a loving earthly father would extend to his
family, God gives to us and a thousand times more. He does not leave
the understanding of His will to conjecture. Rather, He has stated
clearly what He wants us to do. It is up to us to put ourselves in the
right place, for it is there that we can be used by God.

Go with What You Already Have

The success of the little boy's involvement in the miracle which Jesus
performed is in the fact that he was willing to offer what little that he
had. All too often, people fail to respond to God by faith because they
believe that what they have to offer Him is so insignificant that God
could not use it.

When Andrew brought the boy to Jesus with the barley loaves
and the fish, he said, "But what are they among so many?" While
Andrew should be commended for at least bringing the boy and his
lunch to Jesus, he still expressed his own doubt as to the significance
of such an offer.

Like so many of us, Andrew temporarily forgot that he was speaking to the Creator Himself. This was not some simple rabbi who
could do little more than divide it among a handful of people. This
was the very One who could bless and multiply the offering so that it
would adequately feed a great multitude of people.

How many times do we feel that what we have to offer God is so
small and insignificant that it will make very little difference?

When we focus on our inabilities and fail to focus on His ability, we can feel that our service to God is worthless. In a very real sense, we *are* worthless, in and of ourselves. But when we offer even our most inadequate service to God, He has promised to bless and multiply it beyond our wildest expectations.

> *You do not have to become great to do great things for God.*

Think of all the people in the Bible that God used in spite of their shortcomings:

- Gideon was a coward who was afraid of his own shadow, yet God turned him into a mighty warrior and leader of Israel.
- David was just a teenager when he stood before the mighty Goliath, yet when the opportunity presented itself for him to stand against the great Philistine warrior, he went forth without armor, taking with him only a small sling and five stones.
- Isaiah, the prophet, said that he was unclean and unfit for the ministry, yet God used him to write one of the greatest books of the Old Testament.
- Paul called himself the "chief of sinners," and despite his early resistance to the message of the gospel, he became the greatest gospel preacher who ever lived.
- Peter bitterly denied the Lord the night before His crucifixion, but he later preached one of the greatest sermons ever given.

God is not looking for people who want to make a difference by their own effort. He is looking for those who are willing to go and serve Him with what abilities or inabilities they already have.

You do not have to become great to do great things for God. Just offer yourself to Him and follow the dream He has placed in your heart. Stop waiting for God to put something you consider "special" into your hand before you offer Him that which is already there.

Give God All That You Have

We are not told what thoughts must have gone through the mind of this boy as he offered his lunch to Andrew, who in turn offered it to Jesus. If he had been like many Christians today, he would have eaten half of the lunch and offered the other half to the Savior.

Unfortunately, that is how many of us operate. We will give God Sunday morning, but we won't give Him Sunday night. We will think about what we ought to put into the offering plate and then give about half that amount.

The wonderful thing about this lad is that he offered his *entire* lunch. Likewise, we must be willing to give to God and hold back nothing; only then will we experience His power at work in our lives. Just as the boy gave Jesus all that he had and the Savior blessed it and multiplied it, so will He do for you and me.

God deserves our very best. In light of all that He has done for us, He deserves our all. The Bible reminds us that God so loved the world that He gave us His Son; He gave us all that He had to give. How can we do less than give Him our very best as an act of surrender and service to Him? How can we hold back anything from God when He has given His only begotten Son for us?

> *The greatest possession that you have is not your money or your job. It is the eternal relationship which you have with the living God.*

The greatest possession that you have is not your money or your job. It is the eternal relationship which you have with the living God. Money may come and go but Christ alone is everlasting. You may have knowledge and wisdom, but remember, within the next ten years or so, much of your knowledge will become outdated. In God, however, you have the wisdom that surpasses all the understanding of this world—wisdom that will last a lifetime.

You may have a well-ordered life with all the security that this world can provide, but your greatest security is in your relationship to God, not in the things of this world. Real joy and happiness come only from God, not from material possessions.

Imagine the wonderful joy and contentment that the little boy felt when he gave his entire lunch to Jesus Christ. Once he experienced the miracle in his heart, it resulted in the miracle of the feeding of the five thousand.

There is no way that he could have ever imagined what would come from his simple offering. Likewise, you and I cannot imagine what will come from our lives being surrendered to the will and purpose of God.

You Can Make a Difference!

Once our Lord touched the simple offering of the young boy, He multiplied it so dramatically that it not only fed the thousands of people gathered on that hillside, but there were twelve baskets full of leftover food! It was the touch of the Master's hand that changed everything that day. And that is the way it still is today.

One of the most wonderful things in a pastor's life is observing people when they genuinely come to God by faith and surrender what they have to His service. When they give their all, suddenly something wonderful and incredible begins to happen. Inevitably, they become amazed by what God is doing in their lives. I have often heard people say, "Pastor, you just can't believe what is happening in my business (or "in our home," or "in my life"). I never dreamed it could be so good."

Alan and Janice struggled throughout the early years of their marriage. They struggled in their business efforts as well. For years it seemed like nothing really went right for them.

"We couldn't focus on anything," Alan told me, "because our lives were totally out of focus."

"When we finally realized that we had left God out of our lives," Janice explained, "we knew we had to start all over again."

The transformation began when they both committed their lives to Christ. Then they recommitted their marriage vows. Next, they dedicated their business to the Lord. In less than two years, they had a solid marriage and a booming business.

What brings about such wonderful transformations? The principle is the same today as it was when Jesus was on earth. Surrender what you have totally and completely to God's service, and when you do, He will multiply it and use it to His glory!

The story of the feeding of the five thousand ends with the statement, "Then those men, when they had seen the miracle that Jesus did, said, This is of a truth that Prophet that should come into the world" (John 6:14). The miracle was so convincing that the crowd who had gathered to hear Jesus realized that He was no mere teacher or rabbi, but that He was the Prophet of God who Scripture predicted would come and turn the hearts of the people of Israel back to God.

God wants to do the very same kind of work in our lives today. If we are willing to surrender our all to Him and let Him use us to make a difference in our world, the end result will be that people will be attracted to our Savior. When others see what He can do with our lives, how He has helped our dreams come true, they will look beyond us to the One who has made all the difference.

> I've dreamed many dreams that never came true
>> I've seen them vanish at dawn,
> But I've realized enough of my dreams, thank God,
>> To make me want to dream on.

Focus on the Future

1. Take some time to think about your future. Where are you going? How are you going to get there? What will it take to make it happen? What will it cost? When do you plan to get started?

2. Ask yourself these questions and fill in the answers:

   What do I want to be? _____

   Where do I want to go? _____

   What do I want to do? _____

   What goals do I need to set?_____

   _____

   What plans do I need to make? _____

   _____

Remember, few people ever get anywhere by accident. Success doesn't just happen. It is usually the result of a well-ordered plan. It comes from a life that is focused on where it is going and how it plans to get there.

5

Making Decisions and Making Them Work

When I was a child, my father told me a story that taught me the value of making decisions. He told me about two frogs that were hopping through a barn where a farmer was milking a cow. When the farmer finished, he got up to care for one of the animals and left the bucket of milk sitting on the barn floor. The two frogs came upon the bucket and wondered what was inside. One suggested that the other hop into the bucket to investigate.

"I'm not going alone," he replied.

"Very well," responded the other frog, "I'll jump in if you will."

They both took a big leap and landed into the milk. At first, they were splashing around and having a big time. But then, they realized they couldn't get out of the milk bucket. As they began to tire from swimming around, the one frog looked at the other and said, "We might as well give up! We're never going to get out of here!"

"Oh no," said the other frog. "We can't give up now. We have to keep on trying."

"Not me," said the first frog. "I've had enough! I'm going to give up!" Bloop…gloop! Down he went into the milk and drowned.

The other frog kept splashing and kicking, splashing and kicking, until to his amazement, the milk began to curdle. After a while, it became a plug of butter. Then the frog hopped onto the butter and jumped out of the bucket.

My father looked at me and said, "Son, there may be times when you feel like quitting. You may even want to give up altogether. If you do, down you will go. Remember, never give up! Keep on kicking and you will always find a way out!"

Indecision keeps us from action. It spoils our progress and it perpetuates mediocrity. It has often been said that all of life is making decisions and making them work!

It is too easy to get into a rut in life and just stay there. Some people are virtual prisoners of their own routines. They are so caught up in doing the same things day after day that they have little or no time to think about the future. Trapped in the cycle of mediocrity, they fail to make decisions.

We live in a pessimistic society. Ours is a "can't be done" world. If you don't believe it, try going to work with a sparkling new idea. Listen as those around you try to quench or squelch it. Even in many of our churches, you will find little vision and excitement or faith in what God can do.

God has unlimited power to meet our needs. But too many of us limit His power with small-minded thinking. Only when we think and act by faith can we overcome the limitations that hold us captive every day.

One of the most incredible stories in the Bible is that of Job. The story is set in the days of the ancient patriarchs. It revolves around the experiences of a wealthy herdsman; it also reveals the spiritual struggle that goes on behind the scenes of Job's life.

> *Indecision keeps us from action. It spoils our progress and it perpetuates mediocrity.*

Job is introduced in the Bible as a man of great wealth and substance. He had seven sons and three daughters and was blessed with seven thousand sheep, three thousand camels, five hundred yoke of oxen, and five hundred donkeys. By today's standard, Job would have been a wealthy man indeed! He would have driven a luxury car and lived in a multi-million-dollar mansion. He was wealthy beyond comprehension in the ancient world.

The Bible also says that he was a righteous man who loved God, goodness, and his family. He was blessed by God and he realized that all he had was a gift from Him. He even used his wealth to bring glory to God.

The story of Job is a story of personal tragedy. In one day, he lost all of his children and all of his wealth. Bandits stole his sheep and cattle. His herds were devastated and his servants slaughtered. Before the day was over, his children were killed in a desert storm.

Devastated by these personal tragedies, Job simply responded, "Naked came I out of my mother's womb, and naked shall I return thither: the LORD gave, and the LORD hath taken away; blessed be the name of the LORD" (Job 1:21).

Later, Job even lost his health. The biblical story pictures him sitting in a pile of ashes, pathetically scraping himself with a broken piece of pottery. He had been reduced to the trash pile of life. Broken and rejected, he still proclaimed, "Shall we receive good at the hand of God, and shall we not receive evil?" (2:10).

Despite all his struggles, Job made some of the most important decisions that anyone could ever make in life. He did not let his faith in God waiver. In spite of his personal pain, he learned to "keep on keeping on" by the grace of God. And because of that faith, God eventually vindicated him, and blessed him with ten more children and twice as many possessions as he had before.

> *When we feel like no one understands, we eventually feel like no one cares.*

The story of Job reminds us to ask ourselves how we are doing with our struggles. Have you been so bombarded by the problems of life that you are ready to give up? Has the rug been pulled out from under you and left you in a heap of ashes? If it has, this is no time to quit!

We all get down at times. And when we do, we start to wallow in self-pity. We tend to think that no one understands our pain or our problems. When we feel like no one understands, we eventually feel like no one cares. If you are discouraged about the struggles of life, let me remind you of three simple principles that can help you get up from the trash pile of defeat and move on.

1. *Hang on to the Promises of God.*
   In Psalm 121:1–2, we read, "I will lift up mine eyes unto the

hills, from whence cometh by help. My help cometh from the LORD, which made heaven and earth."

2. **Rely on the Provision of God.**

   The Bible promises in 1 Corinthians 2:9, "Eye hath not seen, nor ear heard, neither have entered into the heart of man, the things which God hath prepared for them that love him."

3. **Keep your eyes on the Prize.**

   Philippians 3:13–14 urges, "Forgetting those things which are behind, and reaching forth unto those things which are before, I press toward the mark for the prize of the high calling of God in Christ Jesus."

No More Excuses

If you are going to make progress in your life, you have to overcome the excuses for your past failures. I heard someone the other day call it getting rid of the "Yeah, But" card!

"*Yeah,* I know I have great potential, *but* you don't know what I've been through."

"*Yeah,* I know God loves me, *but* it seems like He's forgotten me."

"*Yeah,* I could rise above my circumstances, *but* I was born economically disadvantaged."

"*Yeah,* I could get an education, *but* I'm too busy working."

Every time you face a decision that could improve your future, you pull out your "Yeah, But" card, and charge your potential with your past limitations—and remain stuck in mediocrity!

Monty Roberts tells the story of how he grew up as the son of an itinerant horse trainer who moved from stable to stable and track to track. As a senior in high school, Monty was asked to write a paper on what he wanted to do when he grew up.

He wrote a seven-page paper describing his goal of owning a 200-acre horse ranch. The paper was complete with diagrams of the buildings, stables, and track. Then he added a 4,000-square-foot house that sat right in the middle of the 200-acre ranch.

Monty proudly handed in his paper. But when it was returned two days later, there was a large red F on top of the first page. When he asked why he had received an F, the indignant teacher replied,

"This is an unrealistic dream for a young boy like you. You have no money. No resources. There's no way you could ever do it!"

Then, the teacher told him to rewrite the paper with a more realistic goal. Monty went home and thought about it long and hard. After several days, he turned in the very same paper.

"You can keep the F and I'll keep my dream!"

Years later Monty Roberts framed the front page of the paper and hung it over his fireplace in his 4,000-square-foot house which sits in the middle of his 200-acre horse ranch in San Ysidro, California![1]

Don't let anyone steal your dreams. Get rid of your excuses and keep on dreaming.

Get Focused

A story was printed in an eastern newspaper of a reporter who visited a western town in the nineteenth century. He noticed several targets drawn on the sides of various buildings around town which had been shot right in the bullseye.

Wow! he thought to himself. *Whoever did this must be the best shot in town.*

Seeking an interview with the great marksman, the reporter was directed to the town drunk!

"How in the world did you shoot out every bullseye," the reporter asked, "and be drunk at that?"

"Aw, it weren't hard," said the old man. "I shot first and drew the targets later!"

> *Decision making involves setting goals. You can't get anywhere if you don't know where you're going.*

Unfortunately, that is how many people conduct their lives. Their motto seems to be, "Ready—Fire—Aim." All too often they hit nothing because they aim at nothing.

Decision making involves setting goals. You can't get anywhere if you don't know where you're going. Choices begin with dreams and are formulated into goals. If we don't start dreaming, we will never develop attainable goals.

Theodore Roosevelt once said, "It is not the critic who counts.... The credit belongs to the man who is actually in the arena ... who errs and comes short again and again because there is no effort without error or shortcomings, who knows great devotion, who spends himself in a worthy cause. . . . If he fails daring greatly, he knows his place shall never be with those timid and cold souls who know neither victory or defeat."[2]

The list of those who initially failed, then refocused, going on to success, is incredible:

• Beethoven was such an awkward violinist, he gave up the instrument to write his own compositions.

• Winston Churchill did not become Prime Minister of England until he was sixty-two, after a lifetime of political defeats and setbacks.

• Louis Pasteur was a mediocre student, ranking fifteenth out of twenty-two chemistry students in his university studies.

• Leo Tolstoy, the author of *War and Peace,* flunked out of college.

• Albert Einstein did not speak until he was four years old and could not read until he was seven. His teacher described him as "mentally slow . . . adrift in his foolish dreams."

• Henry Ford went bankrupt five times before succeeding as the world's best auto maker.

• Abraham Lincoln was born in poverty, raised in obscurity, and failed in business. He ran for office and lost for the state legislature, the congress, and the senate before being elected President of the United States.

Each one of these men eventually succeeded because he remained focused on his goals. Each rose to prominence and success because he refused to give up.

Let God Take Over

Spiritual success works in a similar manner. The Bible says, "Be not conformed to this world; but be ye transformed by the renewing of your mind, that ye may prove what is that good, and acceptable, and perfect will of God" (Rom. 12:2).

God doesn't force His will on us. We can choose to accept His will and receive His blessings. Or, we can reject His will and forfeit His blessings. He makes His will available to us, but we must accept it for ourselves.

If you really want to find God's will for your life, surrender your time, talents, hopes, dreams, family, friends, and future to Him. Let go and surrender to His control. Let His priorities become your priorities; and your will shall be conformed to His will.

God never leaves His purposes to guesswork. He clearly tells us what He wants us to do with our lives. His principles for life are laid out in Scripture. He promises to lead us as we prayerfully seek His guidance.

> It may not be on the mountain's height,
> Or over the stormy sea;
> It may not be at the battle's front,
> My Lord will have need of me;
> But if by a still small voice He calls
> To paths I do not know,
> I'll answer, dear Lord, with my hand in Thine,
> I'll go where you want me to go,
> I'll go where you want me to go, dear Lord,
> O'er mountain, or plain, or sea;
> I'll say what you want me to say, dear Lord,
> I'll be what you want me to be.
>
> Hymn, "I'll Go Where You Want Me to Go,"
> —Mary Brown

Follow the Directions

Have you ever started out on a trip, got lost, and *then* took out the map? People do it all the time! No wonder so many of us get lost, waste time, and show up late. We forget to read the map.

Another typical mistake is to start putting something together without reading the instructions. Pretty soon, you've got hundreds of pieces strewn all over the floor and you don't have a clue what you're doing!

Almost everything in life works better if we follow the instructions. When we do, we soon discover there are specific steps of action that will lead us where we want to go.

If we take the proper steps, we can quickly narrow our options and make the right choices.

Finding God's will for your life works the same way. If we take the proper steps, we can quickly narrow our options and make the right choices. Here is how it works:

Interest. God usually begins to reveal His will to us by creating an interest level within us. Unless you become interested in something, you will not likely pursue it. However, there may be several things we are interested in that we may never pursue. God helps us limit our options.

Ability. The next question we must examine is, "Am I really capable of doing that?" I may be interested in becoming a concert pianist, but if I have little musical ability, that is not likely. If God wants you to pursue something, He will give you the ability to do it.

Limitations. We all have certain limitations. They may be physical, mental, social, or financial. But they are very real to each one of us. If you aren't very good at math, God isn't likely leading you to be a math teacher! If you aren't able to become a world class gymnast or swimmer, God isn't likely preparing you for the Olympics. Each of us has to face our limitations.

Motivation. For most of us, this is the real key. A highly motivated person may overcome many of his or her limitations. He or she may be able to maximize their abilities. They may be highly motivated enough to overcome the initial obstacles in their path. But an unmotivated person will never be willing to pay the price of that kind of success.

Spiritual Gifts. The Bible reminds us that God gives us certain spiritual gifts as our inner spiritual motivation in serving Him. Romans 12:6, 8, lists these as

- preaching
- serving
- teaching
- exhorting
- giving
- ruling
- mercy

As you mature in your walk with God, it will become more and more evident which of these you have. God has gifted me with preaching and ruling. I am driven from within by these two gifts; they affect everything I do and the way I do it.

Opportunities. God opens and closes the doors of our lives. When He does, He is giving us the opportunities that He has designed for us in His will. He may not tell you specifically to move to Iowa. In fact, He may open two or three doors of opportunity. You will have to choose one. One thing is certain, however; whatever doors are closed to you aren't His will for you anyway.

Experience. There is no better teacher than experience. The more you do the job, the more you will learn from it. One level of experience will prepare you for another level. As time goes by, you will eventually become skilled at doing your job.

Expertise. Those who succeed at their work, develop an expertise about it. You eventually become so good at what you are doing that you become an "expert" in your field. You can do it better because you've done it longer. With expertise comes confidence and stability. Others start asking you how to do it because you've been there.

Wisdom. The last step is wisdom. It is the ultimate, but it takes the longest to develop. It only comes after a long series of trial and error experiences. Eventually, we learn to do our jobs better because we have become older and wiser. The immature and the inexperienced lack such wisdom. Indeed, they are virtually incapable of it because they haven't walked far enough down life's road yet.

If we line these steps up like a pyramid, we can see how God leads us to know and do His will:[3]

Notice how God continually narrows our options. We may be interested in a dozen things, but we may only have the ability to do six of them. Of these, one may be off-limits to us for some reason. Then, when we examine our motivations and gifts, we soon narrow the list to two or three. Once that happens, we have to look at which opportunities come open to us. Usually, it is only one or two choices.

At this point, we have to prayerfully make our choice. Take the job and see what happens. If we are meant to stay, our experiences will confirm that in our minds. If we stay at it long enough, we will become experts at it.

It doesn't matter *what* we do but *how* we do it. You can become the best truck driver possible. The best mechanic possible. The best plumber possible. The best school teacher possible. The best computer technician possible. The best CEO possible. Whatever you choose to do, become the best you can at it!

Finalize Your Choices

Notice again the pyramid diagram (Ten Steps to Success). It begins at the bottom with our God-given potential. Gradually, our options narrow. By the time the diagram reaches the level of *opportunities,* one is "limited" to those opportunities which God allows to come into his or her life.

At this point we are certainly free to make our own *choices* based upon the six elements of the chart listen under *God-Given Potential.* These are those factors that are predetermined by the sovereignty of God over our lives. They include those matters over which we have no direct control: sex, race, height, weight, basic intelligence, athletic ability, social and cultural background, family environment, etc.

Once we reach the level of *opportunities,* we must start making our own choices: education, marriage, jobs, location, moves, etc. God does not force these decisions. Obviously, His sovereign preparation influences many of these choices, but it does not limit them.

For example, consider this scenario:

GOD-GIVEN POTENTIAL

Bob Smith, born in Chicago in 1975.
Educated in public schools. Accepts Christ at age fifteen.
Non-Christian Parents—Stable Family Environment
Good Student (B+ Average)
Excellent Athlete
Spiritual Gifts: Exhortation and Giving

OPPORTUNITIES

Local: Basketball scholarship offers at two local colleges.
No scholarship offers at local community colleges (low tuition rates).

National: Partial basketball scholarship offer at out-of-state
secular college. (Must work to pay difference.)
Non-athletic Chancellor's Tuition Scholarship offer
at out-of-state Christian university.

What would you do if you were Bob? Chances are your choice will be influenced by your background factors as well. *Outside influences* will play a role also. Take Bob's example and add these factors:

• Parents prefer local community college.
• Pastor recommends out-of-state Christian university.
• Youth pastor prefers local Christian college.
• Girlfriend is going to Christian college in Chicago area.
• Best friend is going to out-of-state secular college.

Now, what choice will Bob make? What choice would you make? Why?

Let's take this process a step further. Assume that Bob makes his choice and attends school X. Once there, his experiences will influence further choices. For example:

• physical health and personal adjustments
• grades and academic performance

- athletic success or failure
- general spiritual and personal growth
- continued outside pressures from parents, friends, mentors

Finding God's will for your life will extend choices you must make regarding education, marriage, jobs, locations, moves, spiritual growth, practical service, etc. As you learn from your mistakes and benefit from your successes, you will gain the *wisdom* to make better choices in the future.

Let's try another scenario:

GOD-GIVEN POTENTIAL

Bill and Jane Johnson live in Dallas, Texas.
Both are Christians—Active in local church.
His family lives in Houston, Texas (Christians).
Her family is in Tampa, Florida (non–Christians).

OPPORTUNITIES

Bill works for computer company.
Jane is a nurse at the local hospital.
Bill is offered a job in Atlanta, Georgia.
Jane is two months pregnant with their second child.
Good local church options in both Dallas or Atlanta.

CHOICES

1. Stay in Dallas. Avoid moving and relocation costs. Cut back expenses to prepare for Jane being out of work after new baby is born.

2. Move to Atlanta. Take new job. Extra income will ease problem of her not working. Fresh start in a new place. Closer to her parents.

What decision will they make? What decision would you make? What decision would your spouse make? Why?

As your expertise and wisdom increase, your choices will improve. So will the potential of your success. Ultimate success is not measured in wealth, possessions, or position, but in reaching your God-given potential. When that occurs, you will experience maximum personal *effectiveness* and maximum personal *fulfillment*.

> *If you make wise choices, based on God's principles, you can be assured of genuine success in the will of God for your life.*

At every stage and age of life, you can make decisions and then do whatever is necessary to make them work to the glory of God. If you make wise choices, based on God's principles, you can be assured of genuine success in the will of God for your life.

Focus on the Future

1. Evaluate your focus. Is it clear? Where are you now? Where do you want to be in the future? Is God in control of your choices? Are you following His directions?

2. What is your spiritual gift? List it (them):

   _____

   _____

   _____

3. What opportunities are open to you right now? Which are you most motivated to pursue?

   _____

   _____

4. What choices do you need to be making now in order to determine your future?

   _____

   _____

6

Help over the Hurdles

Several years ago when my daughter Tonya was a child, I was teaching her the sixty-six books of the Bible. We were going through the Old Testament books, repeating them from memory, when she ran into difficulty. She said, "Isaiah . . . Jeremiah . . . Limitations . . ." "Whoa," I said, "Back up and say that again." "Alright, Daddy: Isaiah, Jeremiah, Limitations."

I smiled and then explained to her that the book was not "Limitations," but "Lamentations." Later, I thought to myself that she may have a good point after all! Too many people act as though they are living by the Book of "Limitations" most of the time. In reality, there is no such book in the Bible! God wrote sixty-six books filled with un-limitations!

God's unlimited power is only limited by our small-minded thinking. Only when we plug in to the unlimited power of God can we overcome the limitations of life itself. As a minister, I am compelled to deal with people every day of my life who are struggling with problems and difficulties of life. Some folks are struggling with the minor issues of life: finances, problems at work, or in the home. Others are facing serious illnesses, the loss of a job, or the death of a loved one. In every case it is my

> *God's unlimited power is only limited by our small-minded thinking.*

great joy to remind them that there is a power greater than themselves who can help them overcome life's greatest hurdles.

I am often reminded of the biblical example of Peter who was captivated by Jesus' ability to walk on the water. When Peter saw the Lord walking on the surface of the lake at Galilee, he called to Him to ask if he could also walk on the water. When Jesus bid him step out of the boat and come to Him, Peter took one of the greatest steps of faith anyone has ever taken. His eyes were transfixed upon the Lord so that he never even noticed the storm raging about him. Peter did something for a few moments that no other human being had ever done before—he walked on the water and defied the Laws of Nature. But as soon as he took his eyes off the Lord and looked at the storm and the raging sea, he began to sink and nearly drowned.

Like many new believers, Peter's step of faith eventually turned into a personal disaster. The enthusiasm of stepping out of the boat was replaced by the desperate need to get back into the boat. His fascination with faith suddenly became a fiasco. His venture into the water revealed his vulnerability. All of a sudden, the miracle became a mess.

Get Your Eyes Off Yourself

We, too, are often tempted to focus on the negatives of life. Somewhere along the road of our spiritual journey we begin to lose our initial fascination with the One who has transformed us. Eventually we begin spending more time and effort on other things than we do on our relationship with the Savior. I am sure there must be technical explanations for how this process develops. But my own observation is this: Whenever we spend more time on other things than we spend with God, we begin to sink into the quagmire of self-interest and self-pity. The great positives of life are turned tragically into the great negatives of life. We become overwhelmed by our inability, rather than being focused on His ability.

We live in a very self-centered world. Some have called this the age of narcissism (self-love). Ours is a self-centered and self-indulgent society. This is one of the major reasons why marriages are falling apart. We have lost our concern for and commitment to others. We care only about ourselves.

This age has also been labeled the "me" generation. People want it all and they want it now. "I want to take care of number one" is what many are saying. They are like the little girl in this familiar poem (author unknown):

> I gave a little party this afternoon at three.
> 'Twas very small, three guests in all,
> Just I, myself, and me.
> Myself ate all the candy,
> While I drank all the tea,
> And I was the one who ate the pie,
> And passed the cake to me.

It's Easier Than You Think

Several years ago a small town in the British Isles built a new jail. Local officials bragged that it was escape-proof. To prove their point, they invited the great escape artist, Harry Houdini, to come and test it out.

The Great Houdini accepted the invitation. He had previously boasted that a jail had not been made that could hold him. He was such an expert at escaping from padlocks, boxes, and even jail cells that none could hold him effectively.

On the appointed day, Houdini entered the cell, and the jailer shut the door behind him. The great escape artist heard the noise of steel against the click of the lock as the jailer slipped the key into place. Once the jailer had gone, Houdini took out his tools and began to work on the cell door. An hour passed, then two. What had worked to open the locks of so many other doors didn't seem to be working at all. Houdini couldn't understand it.

Finally, after admitting defeat, Houdini leaned against the door in fatigue—and the door opened! It seems the jailer never locked the door to begin with. The only place the door was locked was in the Great Houdini's mind!

Oh, that we might let God unlock our minds! Only when we believe He can work on our behalf will we see Him transform the impossible into the possible. It is then

Ours is a self-centered and self-indulgent society. This is one of the major reasons why marriages are falling apart.

and only then that people walk where they have never walked before. It is then that the miraculous becomes reality.

Several years ago I came across this poem which has always challenged me personally about the importance of right thinking and a proper focus:

> If you think you are beaten, you are;
>   If you think you dare not, you don't.
> If you want to win but don't think you can,
>   It's almost a cinch you won't.
> If you think you'll lose, you're lost;
>   For out in the world we find
> Success begins with a fellow's will:
>   It's all in the state of mind.
> If you think you're outclassed, you are;
>   You've got to think high to rise;
> You've got to be sure of yourself before
>   You can ever win a prize.
> Life's battles don't always go
>   To the stronger and faster man;
> But sooner or later the man who wins
>   Is the man who thinks he can.[1]
>   —"Thinking," Walter D. Wintle

You may be facing a serious decision that will take an incredible step of faith on your part. Let me remind you that God is willing to go with you every step of the way. But you must believe that He is there, and start walking with the confidence that He will continue with you until you reach your ultimate destination.

DON'T LIMIT THE PEOPLE OF GOD

DON'T LIMIT
People of God
Person of God
Power of God
Purpose of God

Jesus said, "All things are possible to him that believeth" (Mark 9:23). Notice what Jesus said. He said that all things are possible to those that believe. Who are the believers? The people of God!

Unlimited possibilities are not available to just anybody. They are available only to those who believe.

Unlimited possibilities are not available to just anybody. They are available only to those who believe. This doesn't mean that in and of ourselves we are better than anyone else. It simply means that we have been blessed by the grace of God who has made us His own children by faith. The Scripture puts it like this:

> The Lord thy God hath chosen thee to be a special people unto himself, above all people that are upon the face of the earth. (Deut. 7:6)

> Ye shall be a peculiar treasure unto me above all people. (Ex. 19:5)

> Behold, what manner of love the Father hath bestowed upon us, that we should be called the sons of God. (1 John 3:1)

What promises! Sons of God. Peculiar treasures. Special people. We have unlimited potential because we have an unlimited God. There is no excuse for us to live with the same pessimism, worry, fear, and doubt as those who don't know God. God said that we are His special people and we ought to live like it. We have the potential to face the greatest obstacles of life with the greatest confidence of all—God Himself!

Such confidence doesn't mean arrogance. There is no place for pride or self-righteousness in the life of the believer. In fact, the Scripture often goes to great length to condemn such pride and self-sufficiency. Rather, there is a fine balance between genuine humility and dynamic faith. Those who make the greatest difference in life are those who keep both extremes in proper balance. Faith doesn't have to lead to foolishness, but humility doesn't have to lead to defeat either. Some people are so arrogant, they're awful. But others are so humble that they're almost worthless.

When I was doing my undergraduate work at Mercer University, I attended a Head Start Program for children in downtown Atlanta. It was held in an inner-city church and run by some wonderful teachers. While I was there, I spent a lot of time observing one particular teacher. Every morning she would come in and say, "Alright, children, say this: 'I am somebody.'" The little children would repeat, "I am somebody." She continued this every day until the children firmly believed what they were saying.

There was no doubt in my mind that the teacher was not trying to promote self-centeredness or arrogance. Rather, she was trying to help the children develop a proper self-concept. She wanted to help them understand that they were somebody! I believe we can thank God for the assurance that we, too, are somebody through Him.

The Bible is filled with examples of God using people to accomplish His will and purpose:

- Abraham stepped out by faith to find the promised land.
- Moses led the children of Israel out of bondage and into freedom.
- David slew a giant and went on to establish a kingdom.
- Solomon ruled in wisdom and reached the pinnacle of prosperity.
- Daniel stood alone and survived the lions' den.

God is certainly capable of working alone, but He often chooses to work through His people. We are the instruments of His grace and the implements of His power. Never underestimate the power of the people of God.

A few years ago when the movie *The Last Temptation* incensed the sensibilities of Christians all over America, I felt led to make an appeal through our *There's Hope!* broadcast, encouraging God's people to respond to a petition protesting the film's release. In his powerful book *Hollywood vs. America*, Michael Medved graciously tells the story of our involvement in protesting that blasphemous movie.[2] We were able to collect more than 135,000 signatures on the petition and delivered them to the doorstep of Universal Studios. While the major Hollywood studios offered formal support for Universal's position on the matter, the American public voted with their feet and stayed away from the movie in massive numbers. Within a few days, the insidious film was history. God's people made a difference by rallying together in opposition to this public display of blasphemy.

While the studio officials at Universal tried to belittle our attempt, I later learned that it made a tremendous impact at the highest levels of the organization. A dear friend of mine, who works inside the Hollywood movie industry, later told me that three or four more movies were being discussed that also blasphemed the Lord Jesus. But each one was scratched because the producers did not want to deal with the kind of outcry they received from *The Last Temptation*. Sometimes we can make a difference even when we aren't sure we can. God can multiply our efforts to overcome our obstacles. He can do incredible things through us when we are willing to be used by Him.

Don't Limit the Person of God

Most of us don't make a deliberate practice of trying to limit God. We do it by default. We try to conform Him to our small ideas of who He is. We project onto the Creator of the universe the same human limitations that we experience when facing the problems of life ourselves. We act as though God really isn't God. We approach our problems as though they're really greater than He is. This limits our faith, and our lack of faith limits our ability to focus on the possible instead of the impossible.

God can multiply our efforts to overcome our obstacles.

How big is your God? Is He really big enough to help you overcome the greatest limitations of life? In Psalm 19:1, the Scripture says: "The heavens declare the glory of God; and the firmament showeth his handiwork." Consider the awesomeness of the created world around you. The vastness of the heavens alone is almost beyond comprehension.

If you were to travel at the speed of light (186,282 miles per second), in two seconds you would reach the moon. It would take you eight minutes to reach the sun. In four months, at the speed of light, you would finally leave our solar system. It would then take you five years at that speed to reach the nearest star, Alpha-Centauri. If you wanted to exit from the Milky Way Galaxy, it would take you 100,000 years. If you wanted to visit the next galaxy, the Great Nebuli, it would take you 1.5 million years at the speed of light. In fact, you could travel at that speed for 4.5 billion years and never leave the universe. How did God create such a gigantic universe? He created it to declare His glory and to convince us of the magnitude of His power. At the same time, that God loves you personally. He knows your name, feels the beat of your heart, and hears your every prayer.

Men and women of faith have made a difference in our world because they believed that God was greater than they were. They reached beyond normal human limitations because they placed no limitations on the person of God. They served a God who was bigger and greater than themselves. They were able to face each day with confidence because their confidence rested in God.

> *Men and women of faith . . . reached beyond normal human limitations because they placed no limitations on the person of God.*

When I was a teenager, a local department store in Atlanta used to have a contest. If your name was drawn, you could either choose a small bicycle or you could reach into a jar filled with fifty-dollar bills and grab as many as your hand could hold. One of my best friends won the contest, and I advised him, "Ronnie, go for the dollars!"

"But I want the bike," he said.

"Look at your hands," I reminded him. "You have big hands and long fingers. Go for the dollars!"

Despite my advice, Ronnie chose the little bike. I never forgot that incident. Ronnie made a safe choice, but he made a self-limiting choice. He could have grabbed enough dollars to buy several bikes. But like many of us, he settled for less when he could have had more.

God has the potential to give you all you need to meet every need in your life. But you must be willing to reach out with the hand of faith and take it for yourself. Your only limitation is within your own mind. An unlimited God makes an unlimited potential available to everyone who will take it by faith.

Don't Limit the Power of God

God is all-powerful. Theologians use the term *omnipotence*. He is not only greater than us in His person, but also in His power.

One of the most interesting stories in the Bible is found in 2 Kings 6. It is the story of the prophet Elisha and his servant. The prophet's preaching had angered the king of Syria, who gathered his armies and sent them to invade Israel. The troops marched out of Syria during the night and surrounded the little town of Dothan before sunrise. As Elisha's servant got up early in the morning to do his chores, he saw the mountains filled with soldiers and chariots and his heart was stricken with fear.

The trembling servant ran back into the house and told Elisha what he had seen. Elisha put on his garment, walked out, and looked about him. As he saw the troop surrounding the city, his heart leaped within him. The prophet saw something no one else saw that day. Turning to his servant, he said, "Don't be afraid! For our army is bigger than theirs!" (2 Kings 6:16, TLB). Elisha then prayed that God would open the servant's eyes that he might see. As a result, he was able to see the army of heaven and its multitude of horsemen and chariots of fire round about Elisha.

How often we limit the power of God. We are limited by human eyesight that fails to look at the problem through the eyes of faith. We need to remember that we are never alone. We are always surrounded by the army of God. His power and resources are always at our disposal. He is there to help whenever help is needed.

Don't Limit the Purpose of God

God has one great purpose for our lives and that is to bring us to Himself. There is an interesting story in Scripture about a father who brought his demon-possessed son to Jesus' disciples and asked that they cast the demon out of him. Apparently the disciples said what they thought they were supposed to say, did what they thought they were supposed to do, but to no avail. When Jesus appeared on the scene, the father ran to him and explained that he had brought his son to the disciples but that they could not minister to him.

Jesus then responded, "Bring him unto me" (Mark 9:19). He was reminding the father, even as He so often has to remind us, that He alone is the solution to our problems. The biblical story goes on to say that when the boy was brought to Jesus, he fell on the ground in convulsions. Then Jesus took him by the hand, "and lifted him up;

and he arose," (v. 27). The boy was healed by the miraculous power of the Lord Jesus in response to the faith of the boy's father.

Many of us are facing difficult circumstances as well. You may be threatened by personal problems, financial disasters, physical heartaches, or spiritual disappointments. No matter how deep or complex the problem, God is able to meet your needs.

Recently, one of our television viewers wrote me concerning this very thing. She was struggling with the personal pain of rejection she had recently experienced.

> Dear Dr. Lee:
>
> I'm a young mother of two small children who is going through a terrible divorce. My husband left me for another woman about three months ago, and my heart feels like it's about to break apart. I want to believe God is big enough to help me and get my kids and me through this problem. I really do, but I wonder if anyone is that great—even God. Please help me to understand. I've just got to have somebody's help.
>
> Sincerely,
Debbie

As I read Debbie's letter, I understood the depth of her pain. At one time or another we have all found ourselves in some dark valley of despair and wondered if God was really big enough to rescue us. It is not a matter of doubting Him, nor insulting His grace, it's just that in that moment our problems seem to overwhelm our very being. The difficulties can so easily overshadow our faith in the eternal God.

But just when we need Him most, God is always there to remind us that He still cares about our deepest needs. We have not been abandoned. Rather, we have fallen into the hands of a merciful heavenly Father who is shaping us into the very image and likeness of His dear Son.

Bill and Gloria Gaither have expressed it like this in one of their songs:

> Something beautiful, something good
> All my confusion, He understood.

All I had to offer Him was brokenness and strife,
But He made something beautiful out of my life.

The Bible expresses it like this: "The spirit of the Lord God is upon me . . . to comfort all that mourn . . . to give unto them beauty for ashes . . . everlasting joy shall be unto them" (Isa. 61:1, 3, 7).

Jack Hayford comments on this same process in his book *The Power and Blessing.* He writes, "Jesus understands those times, when in the midst of such thirstiness, you also cry out, 'My God, why have you forsaken me?' Our Savior is very akin to our times of travail—when our sense of aloneness and dryness cries for refreshing."[4]

The more desperate our circumstances, the more desperate our faith needs to be. When we get into a situation when we must have God's help, we suddenly learn how to put our faith into action. It is then that we learn to approach the Savior with the kind of faith that says: All things are possible to him that believes! Faith and prayer go hand in hand. Our faith causes us to cry out to the One who alone can help us.

Joseph Scriven was a young man who fell deeply in love with a beautiful girl. All he could think of was her. But the day before their wedding, the girl drowned in a boating accident. Joseph was distraught with bitterness and despair. For several months he questioned the wisdom and purpose of God.

After many days of agony, Joseph realized he had no one to turn to but God Himself to regain his peace of mind. Later, Scriven sat down and wrote the words of this familiar hymn:

> *The more desperate our circumstances, the more desperate our faith needs to be.*

What a friend we have in Jesus,
All our sins and griefs to bear,
What a privilege to carry,
Everything to God in prayer.

Oh, what peace we often forfeit,
Oh, what needless pain we bear,
All because we do not carry,
Everything to God in prayer.

Until his death in 1958, my uncle George Hitt was a silhouette artist of world renown. He would use a special black paper and, through the process of his own imagination, create a beautiful scene that he wished to bring forth. With no preliminary drawings he would envision the finished product in his mind. George would use surgical scissors to cut the silhouette with all its intricacy out of the black paper. The results were amazing. Pictures seemed to come to life out of the page.

He might make a silhouette of a dancer gracefully moving across the stage, a deer standing in a flowery meadow, or even the portrait of some famous individual. In fact, it was his skill in portraits that caused President Franklin D. Roosevelt to invite George to the White House to do silhouette profiles of the entire Roosevelt family.

During his lifetime, George was proclaimed by many to be the greatest silhouette artist in the world. *Guidepost* magazine ran stories on his accomplishments, and Robert Ripley made him a topic of *Ripley's Believe It or Not*.

But what was so special about George was not just that he was a great artist. Nor that he had received great acclaim. But the fact that since he was a seven-year-old boy he had been severely crippled by rheumatoid arthritis. His head, arms, legs, and feet were held rigid in the vise-like grip of this incurable disease.

Confined to his bed or his wheelchair, he could not feed or dress himself. The only movement he had in his body was the slight use of his left arm and thumb. Yet with the special surgical scissors placed tightly between his thumb and index finger, he reproduced scenes and characters in silhouette with unbelievable precision and reality.

In George, God had chosen to make the impossible possible. Uncle George's favorite saying tells it all, "Don't worry about what you think you can't do. But with all your heart and soul do those things that God wants to do through you." What he meant was: There are no limits to what God can do through us!

Focus on the Future

If all things are possible to those that believe, what do I need to believe God for in my life right now? How will that belief affect my future? Can I really trust God with my personal problems? Which problems? Make a specific list! Don't limit the power of God in your life. Fill in your list.

1. _____
2. _____
3. _____
4. _____

Now, hold this list up to God in prayer. And claim His power to meet your needs. Remember, all things are possible to those who believe! Now, make a separate list of the steps of faith you need to take in order to make these possibilities a reality.

1. _____
2. _____
3. _____
4. _____

7

Learning from Our Mistakes

Russell Conwell, for whom Gordon-Conwell Divinity School is named, used to preach a famous sermon, entitled "Acres of Diamonds."[1] In it, he told the famous story about a man who lost everything in search of a great treasure. Ali Hafed lived near the Indus River in ancient Persia. One day an old priest visited him and, among other things, told him, "A diamond is a congealed drop of sunlight." The old priest informed him that if he had one diamond the size of his thumb he could purchase the county. If he had a mine of diamonds, he could place his children upon thrones. That night Ali Hafed went to his bed a poor man. He had not lost anything, but he was poor because he was discontented. And he was discontented because he feared he was poor. He said to himself, *I want a mine of diamonds.* All that night he lay awake restlessly thinking.

Early the next morning, he sought out the priest: "Will you tell me where I can find diamonds?" "Diamonds! What do you want with diamonds?" "I wish to be immensely rich, but I do not know where to go." "Well," said the priest, "if you will find a river that runs through white sands, you will always find diamonds." Ali Hafed said, "I do not believe there are any such rivers." "Oh, yes," replied the priest, "there are plenty of them." So Ali Hafed sold his farm, collected his money, and left his family in the charge of a neighbor.

Ali set off in search of diamonds. He started at the Mountains of the Moon. Afterwards he came around to Palestine. Then he wandered on into Europe. At last, when his money was all spent and he was in rags and poverty, he stood on the shores of the Bay at Barcelona in Spain. A great tidal wave came rolling in between the pillars of Hercules, and the poor, afflicted, suffering, dying man could not resist the awful temptation to cast himself into that incoming tide. He sank beneath its foaming crest, never to rise in this life again. But that is not all of the story.

One day the man who purchased Ali Hafed's farm let his camel into the garden to drink. As the camel put his nose into the shallow water of that garden brook, Ali Hafed's successor noticed a curious flash of light from the white sands of the stream. He pulled out a black stone and took the pebble into the house and put it on the mantel. A few days later, the same old priest came to visit the man who had purchased Ali Hafed's farm. The moment he opened the drawing-room door, he saw a flash of light on the mantel. He rushed up to it and shouted, "Here is a diamond! Has Ali Hafed returned?" "Oh, no," his friend said, "Ali Hafed has not returned, and that is not a diamond. That is nothing but a stone we found right out here in our own garden."

"Yes," said the priest, "but I know a diamond when I see it." Together they hurried out into the garden and stirred up the white sands with their fingers. And there came up other more beautiful and valuable gems than the first. Thus was discovered one of the most magnificent diamond mines in all history! Had Ali Hafed remained at home and dug in his own garden, he would have had diamonds in abundance, for every acre of that old farm revealed gems which since have decorated the crowns of monarchs.

For most of us, the answer to our problems is within our grasp. The solution is always closer than we think. All we need to do is look for the answer. Even when God seems silent, He is still speaking to us.

When God Is Silent

What happens when we can't hear God speaking? When all seems silent? Have you ever felt totally alone? Have you ever thought, *Where is God when I need Him?* I'm talking about those times when you have done all you knew to do and there still was no answer from God. Such times of spiritual loneliness come, not only when we have failed God, but when we are doing the very best we know to serve Him as well as we can.

I have certainly felt that way at times in my own life. I knew that Christ lived within me and I was at peace with God. Yet I seemed to be wrestling with the whole issue of God's presence in my life. I was busy serving God, yet He seemed to be silent in all my busyness and activity. It is in such times of personal struggle and spiritual depression, that we need to be reminded that God is still at work in our lives. His sanctifying process is still being accomplished. He is conforming us to the image of Christ whether we realize it or not.

Reasons for God's Silence

There are several reasons for God's silence, and each points to a different aspect of His work of grace on our behalf. Each confronts a different aspect of our spiritual progress. And each is designed to draw us closer to Him.

We are too busy to listen. There are times when God is silent because we are not listening to what He has to say. He sees all the hustle and bustle in our daily routine and realizes we would not hear Him even if He did speak to us. Our lives are so filled with rushing here and there that we rarely take time to be quiet and seek His face.

Busyness is not godliness. It may be a necessity, but it is an activity that will control us if we do not learn to control it. All too often we are too busy to pray, too busy for church, even too busy for our own families. In each of these situations we are certainly too busy for God!

Quiet contemplation is not exactly one of the virtues of modern society. We tend to do more because we have more. All our time-saving conveniences and modern devices only cause us to try to do more instead of less. Since we can go great distances quickly, we are going more but enjoying it less. I don't mean to imply that activity is wrong. On the contrary, we have a God-given mandate to work. Industriousness is a virtue which God blesses. But when activity becomes an end in itself, it will usually rob us of our personal and spiritual vitality.

> *There are times when God is silent because we are not listening to what He has to say.*

Recently, I was talking to a man of some renown. I began to express something to him that was very heavy upon my heart. We were in a crowded room, and I tried my best to gain his attention. As I talked, he kept glancing around the room. His eyes darted everywhere as though he were looking for someone important. He even greeted several people who passed by as I was talking to him. Finally, I gave up in utter frustration. I stopped talking and quietly walked away. Why did I quit? Because he wasn't listening!

Unfortunately, that is how many of us treat God. We are so busy that we don't take time to listen to what He has to say. We don't have any real time for God. Our personal relationship with Him is way down at the bottom of our list of priorities.

The Bible reminds us, "And ye shall seek me, and find me, when ye shall search for me with all your heart" (Jer. 29:13). Finding God's answers to life's toughest questions is a matter of the heart. Sometimes He is silent because He has found us so busy that He is not about to reveal Himself to us. "Be still, and know that I am God" (Ps. 46:10), the Scripture reminds us.

Oswald Chambers explained, "Watch where God puts you in darkness, and when you are there, keep your mouth shut. . . . Darkness is the time to listen and heed. If you talk to other people, you cannot hear what God is saying. When you are in the dark, listen and God will give you a very precious message for someone else when you get back into the light."

We have already said no. There are times when God is silent because He has spoken to us before and we have said no to His will. There-fore, He withdraws new direction until we have acted upon previous direction. Only when we act upon the truth we already know, will He give us more truth.

I have always been intrigued by the story of Jonah. Most of us have heard the story of his famous ride in the great fish. But few people remember the real point of the story. God told Jonah to go to Nineveh, the capital of Israel's enemy, Assyria. He further instructed him to preach God's message of judgment and call them to repentance. Instead, Jonah turned in the opposite direction and sailed westward out to sea. He ended up spending three nights in the belly of the fish because he had already said no to the will of God for his life.

If God has spoken to you about a specific matter in your life, don't try to rationalize your way out of it. If you say no to God, He may not speak to you on that matter again. Sometimes He stops speaking because no one is listening.

God is putting our faith to the test. There are many times in my own life when God's silence stretched my faith and caused me to grow. I could pray and plead His promises, but He was still silent. And the silence became deafening. In those moments all you can do is take hold of the rope of faith, tie a knot in the end, and hang on for dear life!

In those dark and lonely moments, we must come to grips with the reality of our faith. When all else fails, faith hangs on to the end. Think of the great men and women of God who trusted Him despite their circumstances:

- Abraham believed he would receive the promised land even though it never became a reality in his own lifetime.
- Job trusted God despite losing his children, his fortune, and his health.
- Joseph remained faithful though he was sold into slavery, falsely accused, and sent to prison.
- Moses gave up the riches of Egypt to become the servant of God.
- Gideon overcame his cowardice to win a great victory.
- David abandoned himself to God even though Saul sought to slay him.
- Peter overcame the failure of his denial and publicly proclaimed that Jesus was the Christ.
- Paul survived imprisonment, shipwreck, and persecution to win the world to Christ.

God is getting our attention. Silence is so quiet that it shouts at us. Its unuttered roar is often deafening! Have you ever noticed how quickly silence gets attention? Enter a noisy room, and let it suddenly become quiet, and everyone will notice.

That is why God uses silence to get our attention. When He has spoken to us time and time again and we don't listen, He often resorts to silence. He may withdraw His voice from your soul so you will begin searching for Him all the more intently.

> *Silence is so quiet that it shouts at us. Its unuttered roar is often deafening!*

Believe it or not, there is a sound to silence. It speaks louder than a thunderous roar. We may have been too preoccupied with our own interests to notice it at first, but eventually we realize that God is no longer speaking because we are not listening.

His silence does not mean that He has withdrawn Himself or that He is denying our request. The late Oswald J. Smith was one of the great missionary-minded pastors of the twentieth century. As a young man, he wanted to go to the mission field. But God never gave him any specific direction. He was willing to go to Africa, Asia, or wherever God might send him. Since God remained silent, Dr. Smith went to Toronto, Canada, to establish the People's Church. Instead of sending him to a specific field, God led him to build one of the greatest missionary-sending churches of all time. Today there are thousands of missionaries encircling the globe because God was silent to a young preacher named Oswald J. Smith.

Every Crisis Is an Opportunity

A crisis can push us to spiritual growth, or bring us to the brink of spiritual collapse. The Chinese word for "crisis" is a combination of the symbols for "danger" plus "opportunity." In each crisis, there is both the opportunity for growth and the potential for failure. Our response to the crisis determines whether it will become a building block or a stumbling stone in our lives.

> *A crisis can push us to spiritual growth, or bring us to the brink of spiritual collapse.*

I once heard an amusing story that brings home this point. Once there were two young men deeply in love with girls they were going to marry. One of the men had his bride-to-be leave him for another man. Distraught and unable to handle his crisis, he leaped off a bridge and ended it all. The other young man had his bride-to-be break his heart as well, but in his time of heartache and crisis, he wrote a country music song and made a million dollars! You see, it's all in the way we handle it.

Everyone faces trouble sooner or later. Being a Christian does not automatically make us immune to crises. While our relationship with Christ certainly ought to help us face our problems more effectively, it does not guarantee us a crisis-free life. In fact, the Bible virtually promises us we are going to have trouble. It reminds us this world is no friend of grace. Our lives are never all success and no failure—all mountaintops and no valleys. Everyone of us will face times when we are up as well as times when we are down.

While the Bible clearly teaches we will often face trouble in our lives, it also reminds us we do not have to go out of our way to look for it. For most of us, trouble generally comes unexpectedly. It is not something for which we can plan or prepare. In fact, the greatest crises of life tend to come at the most inopportune times. The telephone rings in the middle of the night, and you are told the awful news of some tragedy. Or your doctor explains you have some serious illness. Or the teacher sends home a note to explain there have been problems at school with your child. As a pastor, I have often seen lives that were permanently changed in one day as the result of some personal tragedy.

How Crises Can Bring Glory to God

The Christian life is one of facing problems, not running from them. In our greatest moments of trouble, we need not fear nor panic because the power of God's Spirit will enable us to endure the crisis. Let me suggest three steps which may be of help in facing crises of life:

Your crisis will help you discover who you really are. What comes out of an orange when you squeeze it? Most of us would say, "Orange juice." But the truth is, whatever is in it is what comes out—seeds and all!

Whenever we are squeezed by life's pressures, whatever comes out of our lives is evidence of what is within us. In a moment of crisis, we either rise to the occasion, or collapse under the pressure. The crisis has a way of helping us understand who and what we really are. It forces us to take a more honest look at ourselves than we normally would. And it also encourages us to realize that whatever our inadequacies, God can meet our needs.

> *The Christian life is one of facing problems, not running from them.*

In life's trying moments we gain a greater insight into our own strengths and weaknesses. If your struggle reveals an area of need in your life, don't run away from it. Face it! Determine to profit from your mistake. If the crisis strengthens your faith and gives you a greater determination to serve God, despite the troubles, thank Him for it!

Your crisis will force you to God. I have never been able to understand why people turn their backs on God at the very moment they need

Him the most. In every time of trouble there comes a point of decision that determines our future destiny. We can either allow our problems to make us better or bitter—the choice is up to us.

I can't help but think of Job. He never once turned away from God though he was bombarded with one crisis after another. Who among us has ever had the kind of problems he had? He lost all of his children and all of his possessions in one day. If that were not enough, he lost his health the next day. But despite the circumstances, Job's faith remained steadfast. "Though he slay me, yet will I trust in him," he proclaimed (Job 13:15).

When the greatest difficulties of life confront us, they will always remind us there is a source of strength beyond ourselves. The power of God is far greater than we ever imagined to meet our needs. When the difficulties come, turn your attention heavenward. And our faithful God will make a path and show you the way.

In a little known part of Switzerland there is a village by the name of End der Welt. In the English language it is translated the "End of the World." This name came because the village is surrounded by high mountains and the road that runs through the village stops on the other side at the base of a steep, rocky cliff. At first sight it looks like you have come to the end of everything with no possibility of going farther. But hidden away in the rocky cliff is a narrow road that leads across the mountains ahead. The village guide is there to show strangers the way.

So it is in our lives. We often are "strangers" on life's journey who seem to reach the "end of our world." But if we look through eyes of faith, our Lord will show us the road ahead. God's way will always lead you to Him.

Your crisis can become a testimony of God's grace. Whenever we face the difficulties of life, others are watching us. Husband, wife, child, friend, or relative—someone is watching your life right now! They may not always notice your reactions when things are going smoothly, but when you remain faithful to Christ—even when everything has gone wrong—you will get their attention.

While we should never try to bring such difficulties upon ourselves, we must recognize that when they do come, God can use them as a testimony to speak to others. Our faith in Him says to them: "God brought me through my difficulties, and He can do the same for you!"

Our lives are not lived in isolation. We are like an open book being read by those who know us best. It is then, and especially then, that God speaks the loudest. In the crucible of human relationships—in our moment of crisis. God is speaking through us by the very way that we respond to His grace which enables us to endure the crisis and rise above it!

Overcoming Our Failures

One of the greatest crises of life is human failure. Its debilitating impact can crush your soul, or it can break your heart! The choice will be up to you.

The Failures of Peter

The story of the apostle Peter reveals several reasons why we fail in our walk with God. As we examine these reasons, ask yourself, "Am I failing in any of these same areas?" Let God examine your heart and challenge your life. Remember, a few steps in the wrong direction can lead to disaster.

He followed afar off. Peter failed on the night he denied the Lord because he refused to remain identified with Christ. After the betrayal and the arrest, the Bible says, "And Peter followed afar off" (Luke 22:54). Peter tried to follow the Lord to see what would happen next, but he made sure he kept his distance. He didn't want to get too close to Jesus now because it might cost him something. The problem is, we cannot follow Christ at a distance without losing sight of who He is and what His claims are on our lives.

The Gallup Polls tell us that millions of Americans claim to have had an experience with Christ. But many of them merely give lip service to Him on Sunday. Their lives are not being transformed by Him day by day. There is no spiritual power in their lives. Their children do not respect their beliefs and they are not growing in the grace of God. They may indeed be saved, but they keep their distance to such a degree that no one would ever be attracted to Christ by the level of their commitment.

He followed the wrong crowd. When Peter arrived at the palace of the high priest, he entered the gate and went into the courtyard. The trial was taking place on the balcony of the palace, and everyone in the courtyard below had a clear view of the proceedings. Peter sat down among the servants of the high priest. He warmed himself at the fire, and sat there expecting the very worst. Out of the range of fellow disciples, Peter was mingling with those who hated and despised the Savior. He was sitting with the ones who were determined to destroy everything he claimed to believe.

Whenever you think you can just blend into the crowd, you're seriously mistaken. Yet many professing Christians today are doing what Peter did back then. They're trying to be part of the world without denying Christ. It didn't work then, and it won't work now! It wasn't long until Peter was denying the very Lord he claimed to serve.

If you want to overcome failure you need to take a clear stand for what you believe. Peter thought he was strong, until he got in with the wrong crowd. As soon as he did, the pressure to conform overcame his commitment to serve.

The three denials came quickly, one upon another. Before he realized what he was doing, Peter had denied the Lord three times in succession. Think of it! Here was Jesus' best disciple deliberately denying he ever knew Him. No sooner had the words of denial fallen from his lips than the rooster crowed and Peter's heart sank within him.

Have you ever fallen like that? In a moment of weakness or pressure, you virtually denied Christ in your life. Have you ever lied about your relationship to Him? Have you ever given in to temptation in a moment of weakness? Have you failed in some area of your life and questioned whether God could ever use you again? If you have, then you know that sinking feeling. You know what it's like, wondering whether you can ever get past the past.

Many people are a prisoner of their past. They feel trapped by mistakes and failures that cannot be erased. They question whether going on is even worth it.

Regaining the Future

Failure is never an easy process. It is humiliating and heartbreaking. It hurts both us and others; it is certainly not something to be desired. But when it happens, it need not be the end of all hope. In fact, failure can be the first real step toward success. It can mean the beginning of a whole new life.

The Bible reminds us that Jesus was fully aware of Peter's failure. At the very moment of his third denial, "the Lord turned, and looked upon Peter" (Luke 22:61). As Peter looked at Jesus' eyes, his heart was broken. He could see the love, the hurt, and the disappointment of the Savior looking back at him. Peter repented because he realized he could not escape the Savior's gaze.

Wherever you go, and whatever you do, you can be sure that God is watching. He knows your deepest thoughts and your most hidden secrets. God sees it all. You cannot escape from Him. And you cannot fall beyond the reach of His grace. No matter how great your struggle, God's power is greater.

Remember God's word. As soon as Peter realized that Jesus was looking right at him, he remembered what He had said to him. Unfortunately when most of us have to come to the end of the line, or the bottom of the barrel before we remember God's warnings. When that happens we realize that God was telling us the truth all along. Despite all our mistakes and failures He remains a God of compassion who loves, forgives, and restores us to useful service on His behalf.

Remove yourself from the place of temptation. The Bible says that Peter "went out." It means exactly what it says. He left the comfort of the fire and the crowd of servants and went out into the night alone. As he did, he removed himself from the place of temptation and defeat.

Some people make the mistake of thinking they're strong enough to handle temptation. They go into the very places where they are vulnerable to sin. They let down their guard under the excuse that what they do is their own business. But what we do is really God's business—because we are His children.

As a pastor, I have never dealt with anyone who overcame temptation by giving in to it. Rather, people were finally able to resist temptation, only when they removed themselves from the source of it. Whatever your area of weakness may be, remove yourself from it, or it from you. It is the only way that you will ever be successful.

Repent of your failure. Peter was so broken by the sin he had committed, he rushed out and "wept bitterly" (Luke 22:62). His tears were tears of repentance. They were the evidence of godly sorrow and a broken spirit. His pride was shattered, and in remorse he wept over the wrong he had done. Tears alone are not necessarily proof of repentance. One might cry and never change, but in Peter's case, his tears were the evidence of a heart that was truly broken and a life that was changed by the power of God. In fact, when most of us think of Peter, we think of his great exploits, not of his great failure.

Peter's life stands as a beacon of hope to everyone who has ever failed God. Here was a man who failed in the worst way possible. He vehemently denied that he ever knew Christ on the night of His betrayal, capture, and execution. Yet afterward, he was forgiven and restored to service by the Lord Himself (see John 21).

On the day of Pentecost, the apostle who had denied the Lord stood and spoke of his faith in the risen Christ. Time and time again he risked his life to preach the gospel and thousands were converted.

If you have failed, there is still hope for you. Though your heart may be broken and your spirit crushed, God can mend your broken heart, revive your spirit, and renew your service.

Unlimited Potential

God has unlimited potential for your life. But you will never realize your full potential until you experience the freedom that is available in Jesus Christ and you surrender yourself to His will and commit yourself to His purpose. God has a distinctive purpose for each of our lives that no one else can ever fill. That which He has called you to do is as vital a task as any ever undertaken. You are as important to Him as anyone who has ever lived and, through personal faith in Christ, you have a potential to reach beyond what could be reached in the future. Witness the story of John Newton. Prior to his conversion, he served in the Royal Navy of England as a slave trader. Later, he became a deserter and turned to piracy. His entire life degenerated into stealing, plundering, and selling slaves.

In spite of the personal sin in his life and the depths of depravity to which he sank, John Newton later came face to face with the claims of Jesus Christ and submitted his life to Him. Over a period of time, God transformed him into a preacher of the grace of God. Later, looking back over his wretched life before meeting Christ and realizing the great grace of God which had been extended to him to bring him to a saving knowledge of Jesus Christ, he wrote these immortal words:

> Amazing grace, how sweet the sound,
> That saved a wretch like me.

> I once was lost, but now am found,
> Was blind, but now I see.

In this beloved hymn, Newton emphasized the power of the grace of God moving on behalf of the helpless sinner. He realized that he had been transformed by a power greater than himself and that he had been given a potential which he could never have reached alone.

Time is a marvelous thing. It enables us to gain a better perspective on the activity of God in our lives. Perhaps you can recall a time in your own life when you were questioning whether you would ever make it. But as you look back now, you can see that God was leading you every step of the way.

It is important that we recall the struggling process that eventually brought us through to victory. It will remind us to reach out with compassion and understanding to those who are struggling as well. God has not called us to condemn them for their failures, but to lift them up and help them in their walk with God. A. M. Overton has expressed it like this:

> My Father's way may twist and turn,
>   My heart may throb and ache,
> But in my soul I'm glad I know,
>   He maketh no mistake.
> My cherished plans may go awry,
>   My hopes may fade away.
> But still I'll trust my Lord to lead
>   For He doth know the way.
>
> Tho' night be dark and it may seem
>   That day will never break;
> I'll pend my faith, my all, in Him
>   He maketh no mistake.
>
> There's so much now I cannot see,
>   My eyesight's far too dim;
> But come what may, I'll simply trust
>   And leave it all to Him.
>
> For by and by the mist will lift
>   And plain it all he'll make,
> Through all the way though dark to me
>   He made not one mistake.[2]

God will never forsake His children. You are a joint heir with Jesus Christ. You belong to Him! The failures of the past are meant to drive us on to the successes of the future.

God is at work in your life. He is not limited by your past failures or your present difficulties. Whatever may have gone wrong, or be going wrong, remember He is working to set it right!

Martin Luther once said, "We are not yet what we shall be, but we are growing toward it. The process is not yet finished. But it is going on. This is not the end, but it is the road to all that God has for us."[3]

Your future is brighter than your past because God is at work in your life. He specializes in reversing our failures and overcoming our mistakes. He delights in helping us to become what we could never become by ourselves. We are His craftsmanship—and He makes no mistakes!

Focus on the Future

You cannot move on to the future until you deal with the past. What is it in years and days gone by that is keeping you from realizing God's full potential for your life? Sin? Failure? Mistakes? Short-comings? Inadequacies?

Make a mental list. Item by item.

God specializes in these very things. Confess them to Him. Name them one by one. Ask Him to forgive you and release you from the consequences of the past. Then trust Him to show you His will for the future.

Ask yourself, "If I were really free from these past mistakes, what would I do differently? What dreams and hopes would be mine?"

Keep on dreaming! Your past has been removed. The slate is clean. The time for a fresh, new start is now!

8

Faith for Tomorrow

Everybody wonders about their future. They want to know what the future holds for them and those they love. Most of us wonder about our health, jobs, family, friends, finance, and a hundred other things.

Ultimately there are only two ways to face the future: faith or fear!

If you are looking at the future with faith and confidence, chances are you are looking at the present the same way. If you are facing the future with fear and uncertainty, you are probably doing the same in regard to the present. Our attitude about the future determines our attitude about the present; our attitude about the present often determines our attitude about the future. If you have faith for tomorrow, you probably will have faith for today. But if you have fear about tomorrow, then you're likely to be full of fear about today. The Bible says, "For God hath not given us the spirit of fear: but of power, and of love, and of a sound mind" (2 Tim. 1:7).

How to Face the Future with Faith

Faith for the future depends upon three key elements.

Remember the Past

In the Old Testament the people of God were always reminded to consider what God had done for them in the past. By looking at the hand of God in the past events of your life, you gain greater confidence to trust Him to be at work in your life in the future. When we consider what God has done in our behalf, we ought to have confidence in the future! He loved us. He saved us. He forgave us. And He has given us an inheritance in Christ that is beyond anything we could ever imagine.

Understand the Present

The Scripture is filled with divine principles for knowing the will of God. You don't need a palm reader, stargazer, or a crystal ball to know the will of God. The divine plan of God for your life is laid out in Scripture principle by principle.

Sometimes it is easier to see the hand of God in the past more easily than it is to see it in the present. But we all need to learn to look for the touch of God's grace in our lives every single day. Time and time again, God is moving on our behalf. Don't overlook His daily providential care for your life. Remember, you're not alone. God is with you every step of the way.

Trust God for the Future

I once knew a boy who always read the end of the book before the beginning. When his mother asked him, "Son, why do you do that?"

The boy replied, "Mom, it's better that way. No matter how much trouble the hero gets into, I don't worry because I know how it's going to turn out in the end."

One of the greatest assurances of the Scripture is that it tells us how things are going to turn out in the end. We may have troubles, hardships, and difficulties along the way, but in the midst of them all, we can believe that the best is yet to come. Most of us are willing to trust God with our eternal destiny, but our struggle comes in trusting Him with our immediate future. The same God who can take you on to heaven can get you through life here below as well. Trust Him and see if He will not prove Himself to you in every way.

You don't need a palm reader, stargazer, or a crystal ball to know the will of God.

The Scripture says, "Trust in the LORD with all thine heart, and lean not unto thine own understanding. In all thy ways acknowledge him, and he shall direct thy paths" (Prov. 3:5–6).

If we have faith for the future in light of these basic scriptural principles, we are ready to make and execute our plans for future success. Believing that the hand of God is upon your life, that He is leading you every step of the way, you can walk into the future with great confidence.

In his book *Christian Excellence,* Jon Johnston observes that life is a "race against the clock."[1] By the time we reach middle age, he observes, we try to use up what Mother Nature has given us before Father Time takes it away!

To plan for the future, we have to take the brevity of life seriously. The average man lives about seventy-four years. That is approximately 888 months, 30,148 weeks, 270,000 days, 648,240 hours, 38,894,400 minutes and 2,022,508,800 heartbeats.

Some have described life's brief stages like this:

- Tender Teens
- Teachable Twenties
- Thrilling Thirties
- Fiery Forties
- Fearful Fifties
- Sensible Sixties
- Sinking Seventies
- Aching Eighties
- Shortening Breath
- Death
- The Sod
- God

How to Maximize Your Time

If our time on earth is brief, how can we best maximize that time to the glory of God? The answer may vary from one person to another. There are some that God will call to a life of scholarship. Such persons will spend a great deal of time in study in order to organize their thoughts and present their beliefs more effectively. There are others that God will lead into activities. They, too, must learn to prioritize their decisions and organize their actions to accomplish the results that they desire. Whatever God's calling in your life may be, there are some basic concepts which are essential for each one of us.

Set Your Priorities

What is it that you really want to accomplish in life. As time goes on and God makes that goal more clear to you, it will be necessary to prioritize your life in order to accomplish your goals. This will involve several key steps. Robert Schuller suggests that each one of us writes down his or her "Mission Statement" for life.[2] He suggests that you ask yourself the following questions:

- What would I try to do if I thought I might succeed?
- What goals would I set if I knew I could not fail?
- What price am I willing to pay?
- What sacrifices am I willing to make?

Then he summarizes his advice by encouraging us to ask ourselves three key questions:

1. What could I do?
2. Where could I go?
3. What could I become?

He also suggests that we differentiate between three categories of things which we hope to accomplish:

1. Things I must do.
2. Things I should do.
3. Things I want to do.

Bottom line: Put first things first!

Organize

Personal organization takes our priorities and arranges them according to our realities. If I need to make my mortgage payment by next month, obviously one of my priorities needs to be that of paying my current bills. At the same time I may have a long-range priority of financing a business venture. But I cannot allow the long-range goal to destroy my short-range goals. This not only happens in finances but it often happens in our personal lives as well. How many people have destroyed their own marriage while trying to amass a fortune or succeed at business. Let me suggest some practical steps to help you get organized:

1. Determine what it is you want to accomplish.
2. Determine the order in which you need to accomplish it.
3. Determine what it will cost.
4. Determine if you need help to accomplish your goal.

These are steps only you can make because only you will know what goals you want to accomplish. However, the principles of God's Word are the same for all of us: honesty, sincerity, faithfulness, dependability, and concern for others. All of these must be followed if we are to expect the blessing of God in our lives.

Each one of us needs to believe that God is generally at work in our lives. If we understand who He is, and understand who we are in relation to Him, then we are prepared to face the issues of life realistically and practically.

Practicalize

I am not sure that there is such a word as *practicalize*. What I mean by it is that we must make our dreams come true in practical ways. Each small step will enable us to take a bigger step the next time. We cannot afford to sit around and simply theorize about the future. If we are going to accomplish something by the grace of God, we must begin to tackle it in a practical manner.

Revitalize

Every dream will become stale in time. Every new venture will sap our energy and creativity. Sooner or later, there will come a time in which we must revitalize our vision for the future. This may require a personal renewal of your own spiritual life. It may necessitate an honest evaluation of your past and present progress. It may also necessitate a greater step of faith than you have ever made before.

Revitalization ultimately means focusing on God's will for your life. Insecure people tend to focus on those things that will make them feel better about themselves. Their lives revolve around questions like:

- "What's in it for me?"
- "What will I get out of it?"
- "Would anyone like me better if I do this?"

Selfish people find emotional fulfillment in things. Their approach to life tends to ask and answer the following questions:

- "Unhappy? Buy something new!"
- "Bored? Go shopping!"
- "Fearful? Buy a gun!"

The balanced person will overcome these selfish desires by learning to focus on:

1. God
2. Others
3. Self

The balanced person puts God first, others second, and himself last. Learning to live for God and for others brings true joy and happiness into our lives. When we spend our time and energy trying to make ourselves happy, we usually become miserable! The problem is we are focused on ourselves and our things. We have lost the true focus of God and other people. If you truly want to be happy, learn to live your life in surrender to the plan and purpose of God. And learn to live your life focused on meeting the needs of others.

> *The balanced person puts God first, others second, and himself last.*

Some have expressed this in the following manner: Find a need and fill it!

Ted Engstrom refers to this as, "Making Others Number One."[3] He suggests five crucial guidelines to helping others feel valued.

1. Be a friend to yourself.
2. Be willing to ask questions and then wait for answers.

3. Encourage others in their own personal spiritual and practical growth.
4. Mention your own faults before you begin criticizing those of others.
5. Do your part to create an atmosphere of friendship.

Remember that Grandma used to say: "You can catch more flies with honey than you do with vinegar!"

Eternalize

If we are going to live our lives to make an effective impact on the future, we must live them in the light of eternity.

Stephen Arterburn reminds us all of the importance of focusing on the future in light of the eternal: "We tend to get caught up in all that we do and lose sight of all that is truly important. We get so focused on the busyness that we forget who we are and why we are here."[4] Even secular psychologists, like Erik Erikson, acknowledge that the final stage of life ought to involve integrity and personal fulfillment. Arterburn raises the question: "Try to imagine your thoughts on your death bed. What will you wish you'd done differently?" He calls this "Dying with Character."

People with character ultimately find the greatest fulfillment in life. They are able to look back over their lives and understand that they have lived with honesty and integrity. People with character are concerned about those who will come after them. They are also concerned to leave behind a legacy of a life well lived.

One of the most incredible examples of someone who was able to eternalize effectively is found in the story of Caleb in the Book of Joshua.

People with character ultimately find the greatest fulfillment in life.

The children of Israel had followed Moses forty years through the Sinai wilderness. They had come to the Jordan River and the border of the promised land. Moses had died and Joshua was chosen to succeed him. Among the men of Israel was a man named Caleb who had served with Joshua years before when the two of them helped to spy out the land.

When the opportunity came for them to conquer the promised land, Caleb requested that Joshua give him the opportunity to conquer the city of Hebron. Caleb's heart must have pounded within him as he remembered Moses' promise to give him the mountain city, which was the stronghold of giants known as the Anakim. Caleb wanted to possess that which was rightfully his. But there were incredible obstacles to overcome. The place that Caleb chose was probably the most difficult place in all of Israel to conquer. It was a high mountain fortress city, south of Jerusalem. It would later become the capital city of the tribe of Judah.

Notice the basic steps which Caleb took in light of eternity in order to make his dream become a present reality:

He identified what he wanted. Caleb knew exactly what he wanted. He did not come to Joshua with a vague offer. He specifically stated that he was willing to do whatever was necessary to conquer that mountain city.

Obviously God knows what our needs are before we ask Him. But there is nothing more important than being willing to ask Him specifically. Too many people pray in vague generalities rather than in specific requests. If you have a need, clearly identify your need, and express it to God.

He focused on what he was promised. Even though he had to wait forty-five years for the fulfillment of the promise Moses had made him, Caleb never lost sight of what he was promised. Apparently he had seen Hebron on his first visit to the land of Canaan. This rocky mountain fortress so captured his mind and attention that he never forgot it. Even during those difficult days wandering in the wilderness sands of the Sinai, his heart continued to beat with anticipation of the day when this place would be his.

The key to Caleb's success was not merely in his own determination, but in his firm conviction that God was the source of the fulfillment of the promise. He knew that the promise would be fulfilled because he knew who had made it. A promise is only as good as the word of the one who makes it. Therefore, if God has made a promise to you, then you have every reason to believe it will be fulfilled.

He never stopped believing. Three times in the fourteenth chapter of Joshua we read that Caleb "wholly followed the Lord" (vv. 8–9, 14).

This gives us a key insight into his character. He was a deeply committed individual. During the forty years of the wilderness wandering he watched an entire adult generation die off in the wilderness. He and Joshua were the only exceptions. Yet he never lost confidence in the promise God had made to him.

Too many people have a half-hearted faith that never activates the promises of God.

Too many people have a half-hearted faith that never activates the promises of God. They question the reality of what God has promised, and then toss up a prayer with little or no expectation that it will be answered. Throughout Caleb's life he never lost sight of the promise of God. The most wonderful epitaph that could ever be recorded of any individual is that he or she "wholly followed the Lord." The Scripture states a simple principle: "According to your faith be it unto you" (Matt. 9:29). There's a definite sense in which God responds to our faith. The more you are willing to believe Him, the more He is willing to move on your behalf. The Bible also reminds us that "without faith it is impossible to please him" (Heb. 11:6). Men and women of great faith have always been willing to believe God for the impossible simply because He said it was so.

He made known his request. There is nothing vague about Caleb's request. The words "give me this mountain" made it totally clear to all Israel he was claiming a specific possession. Caleb identified his request to Joshua, the people of Israel, and ultimately to God Himself.

I am convinced we cannot expect God to meet our needs unless we are willing to make them clearly known. This is not because God does not know what our needs are. Rather, it is because Scripture clearly teaches the principle of activating our faith in response to His promises. We do that by making specific requests to God in prayer. The Bible says, "Call unto me, and I will answer thee, and show thee great and mighty things, which thou knowest not" (Jer. 33:3).

Notice that God asks us to call upon Him in order to activate His power in our lives. The New Testament expresses the same concept when it says, "Ye have not, because ye ask not" (James 4:2). Our Lord Jesus said the same thing when He promised, "Ask, and ye shall receive, that your joy may be full" (John 16:24).

He took his possessions. Caleb had been given this mountain by the promise of God. It was his inheritance to claim, but he still had to take hold of the possession personally. There's a great deal of difference between an inheritance and a possession. An inheritance is something someone promises to give us. They may even be legally bound to that promise. But to make your inheritance your possession, you must personally take it for yourself.

Suppose someone had left you a million dollars in an inheritance. He signed all the legal papers to make it guaranteed unto you. You had deposited the money in the bank on your behalf. That would be an inheritance. But it would not become a possession until you went to the bank, withdrew the money, and made use of it yourself.

Caleb was convinced that Mount Hebron was his inheritance. He became ready to go and take possession of it for himself. He engaged the giants in battle and defeated them. From that day until now, Hebron has been known as a place of great determination—one of the most crucial cities in the land of Israel.

Several years ago I read a true story of an incident in the life of the great French conqueror Napoleon. Napoleon and his soldiers overcame an island in the Mediterranean Sea. They had fought for many days to take the island and finally succeeded. After the capture of the island at the price of many lives, Napoleon and his generals gathered for a celebration. As they were sitting around a great table, talking about the victory, they were interrupted by a young officer.

"Let me see Napoleon," he insisted to the guards. But the guards would not let him through. Finally Napoleon himself was so disturbed by the interruption that he told the guards to allow the young man to enter the tent where he was seated, and that he would speak to him personally. The young officer walked into the tent and stood at the end of the table. Looking down the table toward Napoleon, he stood in silence.

Napoleon looked at him and said, "What do you want?"

The young man looked at Napoleon and said, "Give me this island!"

The generals began to laugh. They could not believe he was forward enough to ask Napoleon for the island that they had fought so hard to win. They thought to themselves, *Who does he think he is?* Anyone with the audacity to make such a request of Napoleon was certainly putting his own life at risk.

But then Napoleon turned to one of his aides and asked for a pen and paper. He wrote out a deed to the island, signed it, and gave it to the young man, leaving his generals stunned and amazed.

"How could you do it?" one of the generals asked Napoleon. "What made him worthy to receive this great island?"

"I gave him this island," Napoleon replied, "because he honored me by the magnitude of his request."

We, too, need to honor God by the magnitude of our requests. He does not expect us to live a life of defeat which is far below the standard He had set for us. Neither does He expect us to be satisfied with asking for the crumbs from the table of life. I am convinced that God has made great provisions for us and He expects us to make great requests so that we might experience great joy when He answers our prayers.

The Bible promises, "And this is the confidence that we have in him, that, if we ask anything according to his will, he heareth us: And if we know that he hear us, whatsoever we ask, we know that we have the petitions that we desired of him" (1 John 5:14–15).

Each one of us needs to discover God's divine purpose for our lives. God is not limited to our limitations. He receives all those who willingly surrender their lives to Him. When we become excited about the possibility of life, we begin to understand why God has placed us here in the first place.

> *Each one of us needs to discover God's divine purpose for our lives. God is not limited by our limitations.*

As a young man, I began to get excited about what I could do for God. I made His cause my cause and I made His purpose my purpose. I learned that God had a specific plan for my life. I began to realize I was called of God to serve Him. I also realized that no else could fulfill this service that God was calling me to do.

Once you come to grips with the purpose of God for your life in light of eternity, you'll never be the same again. Helen Steiner Rice said it like this:

Life without purpose
is barren indeed—
There can't be a harvest
unless you plant seed,
There can't be attainment
unless there's a goal,
And man's but a robot
unless there's a soul . . .

If we send no ships out,
    no ships will come in,
And unless there's a contest,
    nobody can win . . .
For games can't be won
    unless they are played,
And prayers can't be answered
    unless they are prayed . . .
So whatever is wrong
    with your life today,
You'll find a solution
    if you kneel down and pray
Not just for pleasure,
    enjoyment and health,
Not just for honors
    and prestige and wealth . . .
But pray for the a purpose
    to make life worth living,
And pray for the joy
    of unselfish giving,
For great is your gladness
    and rich your reward
When you make your life's purpose
    the choice of the Lord.[5]

Making a difference in the world is what life is really all about. The world of our friends, our family, or the society in which we live is part of our God-given responsibility. When we live life in light of His plan and purpose, we realize we count for something because we can make a difference. That is exactly what God has promised us—that regardless of what difficulties may lie ahead, God will use us to His glory!

Focus on the Future

In light of the future, ask yourself these key questions:

1. Past:

What should I have done differently? Therefore, what adjustments will I make for the future? _____

2. *Present:*

What troubles me the most about my life? _____

_____

What pleases me the most about my life? _____

_____

What changes do I need to make? _____

_____

3. *Future:*

Where is my life going? _____

_____

What legacy do I want to leave behind? _____

_____

What do I need to be doing now to insure reaching that goal? _

_____

No one can completely control the future. We can't totally determine our own destiny. But, in most cases, the decisions we make *today* will influence our future success or failure. Remember, there are no shortcuts to the will of God. Every step is sovereignly planned to make us more like Christ and to conform us to God's will for our lives.

9

Taking Responsibility for Your Life

Some have called this "that terrible century!" It was during the twentieth century that the most devastating wars in human history were fought on the surface of this planet—World War I and World War II. It also was the century of the development of nuclear weapons, international terrorism, and the spread of AIDS.

However, the twentieth century has also been a time of incredible development. Many things have been developed to near perfection in the twentieth century:

Telephones	Electricity
Radio	Television
Automobiles	Airplanes
Computers	Satellites
Space Exploration	Medical Advances

Thank God for the incredible changes that have occurred in this century alone. By the end of the first century the message of the gospel had spread into Europe, Asia, and North Africa. Over the next seventeen centuries of human history, it barely moved beyond these parameters. It was not until the fifteenth century that people discovered the world was round. In the sixteenth century they began to explore the continents. In the seventeenth and eighteenth centuries Europeans began to colonize the known world. By the nineteenth century the civilized world was finally fully impacting the uncivilized world. But it was not until the twentieth century that the greatest changes would occur that mankind had ever seen.

We are on the verge of another century! It is almost beyond our comprehension to imagine what changes will occur in our daily lives in the years ahead. But let me assure you that changes will be coming!

Change is a part of life. Living things are constantly developing through a process of change. You are not the same person that you were one year ago—or ten years ago. You have changed and are continuing to change.

The changes of life touch every area of our existence: physical, social, financial, personal, spiritual. Think of all the changes that have occurred in the past twenty-five years: computers, video cassettes, digital watches, microwave ovens, touch-tone dialing, audio-activated answering services, satellite technology, and compact discs. Who could have dreamed of such things back then. But today, they are realities.

We cannot avoid changes, therefore we must learn how to best adapt to the changes which will occur in our lives. A Greek philosopher named Heraclitus once said, "You cannot step twice in the same river." Life is very much like a rolling river. You can never relive a moment, an hour, a day. It is forever changing, forever moving, forever streaming along without a moment's rest.

Yesterday has passed and will not return. Today has come and we must take full advantage of it if we are to influence tomorrow. The future will be the result of the choices and changes that we make in our lives today.

Nobody standing on the threshold of the twentieth century could have conceived of what was to come in the next hundred years: the horrible devastation of World War I, the Depression, Hitler's rise and fall, the Holocaust, the Cold War, the fall of international Communism, and the rise of America as the most powerful and prominent nation in the whole world.

Though many experts claim to, there are few people alive today who really understand or comprehend what lies before us in the days ahead.

It is for that reason that I am reluctant to speculate on the developments of the twenty-first century. Though many experts claim to, there are few people alive today who really understand or comprehend what lies before us in the days ahead. We can only imagine that this will be a century of unparalleled technological advances. The medical world will undoubtedly be in constant conflict with religious and social beliefs as genetic experimentation continues to attempt to provide a better chance for the human species to survive. Some are predicting a century of unparalleled economic growth. Others are forecasting a time of total economic collapse. I am not sure what specifics the future holds in the century ahead, but I can make reliable predictions based on the reality of human nature and the timeless truths of the Word of God.

Deciding Not to Blame

My staff at the church often remind me, "Times change, but people don't!" What they mean by that is that society changes. Culture changes. Styles change. But human nature remains the same.

When most of us get in a mess, we look for somebody to blame. Adam did it to Eve; Eve did it to the serpent. And people have been doing it ever since. We seem to think that blaming our problems on someone else excuses our faulty behavior.

But real change comes when we decide not to blame—when we take full responsibility for our own actions. When we are willing to admit our needs, God is willing to meet our needs. He will move in us when we move toward Him.

The Bible reminds us that man is seriously flawed by the reality of sin. It is that sin that drives our self-centeredness, our greed, our lust, and inevitably leads to our greatest disasters. As long as the vast majority of men and women on this planet do not bow their knee to the Lord Jesus Christ, and allow the Christ of Peace to live within their hearts, there is little hope for true and lasting peace on this planet. If history tells us anything, it tells us that man, left to himself, will eventually destroy himself and everything else in his environment.

Reshaping Our Culture

My dear friend Ed Young has made the observation: "The greatest lie perpetrated today is that God's way does not work. The second greatest lie is that man's way does."[1] In his insightful *Been There. Done That. Now What?*, Ed reminds us that there is no system of values working in this world today but God's system. No other worldview has success-fully taken root which gives meaning and hope to human beings.

We are living at a time today when many young people are ques-tioning the meaning and purpose of life. An entire generation has been raised in our public school system being told that God does not exist. Their views of life, their past and present, are conditioned by the spiritual vacuum in which so many of them live. Those who do not come from Christian homes are devoid of almost any spiritual influ-ence in their lives.

Many of our churches' youth are themselves the victims of the sec-ularization of American society. This process is now running rampant into the new century. Some fear that this may be even the final century of Christian influence in our nation. Certainly many have already undertaken to refer our times as a "post-Christian society."

On the other hand, Cal Thomas argues that we are facing the bankruptcy of liberalism and secularism. He speculates that the un-believer has no permanent solutions to offer. Therefore, he suggests that it is only a matter of time until the liberal-secular agenda is totally bankrupt! In that case, Thomas foresees a tremendous opportunity for Christianity to fill the vacuum that will be left in the heart and soul of America.[2]

Improving Our Personal Response to Change

Change, and the fear that accompanies it, is also *personal*. It is the per-sonal challenge of life's changing landscape with which each of us must deal individually. We may not be able to stop the stampede of the changing culture, but we can certainly deal with the changes in our own personal world. As we face the difficulties of life, each of us is challenged to make a differ-ence in the world in which we live.

> We may not be able to stop the stampede of the changing culture, but we can certainly deal with the changes in our own personal world.

Robert Schuller has reminded us of the importance of putting our problems in their proper perspective in his dynamic book *Tough Times Never Last, but Tough People Do!* Schuller recommends considering these six keys when facing the challenges of life:[3]

1. Everyone has problems.
2. Every problem has a limited life span.
3. Every problem holds positive possibilities.
4. Every problem will challenge you.
5. You can choose what your problem will do to you.
6. There is a negative and positive reaction to every problem.

Let me restate it this way: There is a right way and a wrong way to deal with everything! The Bible is filled with examples of people who had to deal with their failures. But the real losers were the ones who turned against God.

- Cain murdered his brother in a jealous rage and spent the rest of his time running for his life.
- Lot made a selfish choice and it cost him his family.
- Saul turned against God and lost his kingdom.
- Judas betrayed the Lord and committed suicide.
- Ananias and Sapphira lied to God and lost their lives.

Turning Things Around

Life is never all joy and no sadness. While it can be a wonderful and exciting journey of faith, life can still have its own measure of troubles and difficulties. There are going to be those times when such problems enter our lives. You may be sailing along smoothly on the sea of life with everything apparently in order. Then, unexpectedly, we are hit with a disaster.

While it can be a wonderful and exciting journey of faith, life can still have its own measure of troubles and difficulties.

One of the most difficult stories in all of Scripture is that of Joseph. He was despised by his brothers and sold into slavery to a caravan of Arab slave traders. They, in turn, sold him to an Egyptian officer by the name of Potiphar. Despite his circumstances, Joseph remained faithful to the Lord.

Even as a slave Joseph determined to be the best slave he could be to the glory of God. But while he was working in the house of Potiphar, Joseph was falsely accused of misconduct by Potiphar's wife. As a result he was thrown into the royal prison. But even there he became a model prisoner, and was put in charge of the other prisoners.

Despite all of his outward circumstances, and all of the changes which were occurring in his life, God's hand was upon Joseph. In time, he was released from prison and raised to the position of prime minister of Ancient Egypt. He became the Pharaoh's personal advisor. His story is one of the most incredible success stories in all of Scripture.

I have often wondered what thoughts must have gone through Joseph's mind during those difficult days. Surely he must have been tempted to question God. Perhaps he thought that God had turned against him—or that He had even abandoned him. Surely he was tempted to discard his faith and turn to something else. But through all his times of desperation and despair, Joseph remained faithful to God and loved Him.

Perhaps you have recently found yourself in a pit of discouragement as well. You may even be questioning whether God is still with you. It could be you're almost to the point of giving up on life itself. If so, let me encourage you to come to an understanding of your troubles, and to learn how to use them for a stepping-stone to a brighter future.

Many of life's problems are not our fault. While there are certainly problems that result from our own faults, that does not mean that all problems are the result of our own personal mistakes. Some things simply happen that are beyond our control or responsibility. When these things occur, we need not blame ourselves.

Too many people rehash the problems and difficulties of life to the point of their own psychological destruction. You cannot go back and undo the problems that come into your life. You may be able to undo the actions that caused those problems to result, but you can't undo the fact that they've already occurred. Learning to accept problems and facing them confidently in the power of God are two of the most important steps we can ever take to spiritual maturity. This is one of the keys to future success.

You can blame yourself until you're blue in the face. You can always "if" yourself to death in a series of statements like "If I had only done this or that." But that will not remove the problems.

There is a story of a little boy who always had a tendency to blame himself when something went wrong. He was sitting in Sunday

School one day when the teacher decided to ask him a very simple question.

"Where is God?" the teacher asked.

The boy replied, "I don't know."

The teacher looked intently at the boy and said, "Certainly you know where He is! Tell the class where God is!"

Suddenly the boy became so frightened he jumped up and ran out of the classroom. He went down the hall, out the door, and down the street to his house. When he finally got home, he burst through the front door, ran up the stairs to his bedroom, and shut himself in the closet.

The boy's mother ran up the stairs to the bedroom, and tried to get him to come out of the closet. When he refused to open the door, she asked, "What's wrong with you?"

"Oh, Mama," he replied, "you're not going to believe what happened down at the church. God is missing, and they think I did it!"

If you are ever going to overcome the difficulties of life, you must stop blaming everything on yourself. It is time to turn your attention heavenward, and realize that God is still at work in your life. He can even use the life-threatening changes and difficulties that come into our lives for the accomplishment of His purposes.

Life's problems are not God's fault. Some people are quick to blame God for their problems. This is often expressed in questions like:

> "God, why did You take my family from me?"
> "God, why did You let me lose my job?"
> "God, why did You cause me to lose my health?"

Blaming God is not a new tactic. Adam tried it back in the garden of Eden. After Adam and Eve had sinned, they fled into the garden to hide from God. When God came to see them at the end of the day, He asked them why they had eaten of the fruit of the tree. Adam turned to God and said, "The woman whom thou gavest to be with me, she gave me of the tree, and I did eat" (Gen. 3:12). Adam blamed the whole thing on Eve! You might even call it Adam's Law: When things go wrong, blame somebody else.

The Bible is faithful to remind us that God loves us and has our very best intentions at heart. He has promised that He will meet our needs, hear our hurts, and ultimately take us home to live with Him forever. Your life is co-eternal with the life of God. Because He lives, you and I will live forever. That means that God can not only take care of the problems of this life, but He can set them right in the next life as well.

Your present problem is not your final outcome. Joseph was the victim of circumstances. He was sold as a household slave and endured the shame of being sent to the royal dungeon. It wasn't until he was thirty years old that he was released from prison and became Pharaoh's advisor. We know he suffered for fourteen years through one personal disappointment and tragedy after another.

But Joseph understood that God was in control of the final outcome of his life. You and I will never be able to handle the terrible problems of life unless we understand that God really is in control of our lives. Life is not an accident. Life is a daily adventure of living with a personal and powerful God who is active in our daily experiences. If God is for us, who can be against us?

How to Get Out of a Mess

Perhaps even now you have gotten yourself into a mess. Things have gone wrong and it couldn't be much worse. You are not alone. There are millions of people in today's world who feel just as you do. One day everything was going fine. Then, suddenly, the bottom fell out!

No matter how you feel, God can see you through your most desperate hour. Although you're down, you don't have to stay down forever. The whole message of the Bible is one of hope. It is the story of God's love reaching down to the point of our greatest needs.

> *The whole message of the Bible is one of hope. It is the story of God's love reaching down to the point of our greatest needs.*

No matter how many times you have blown it, God still loves you! No matter how complicated or entangled your mistakes may be, there is always a way out—by following the principles of God.

Luke 15 tells us the story of the prodigal son. It's the story of a young man in trouble. He was as far away from God as anyone could go. But the Bible tells us that he came to the end of himself, and realized that only God could provide the answers he so desperately sought.

He wasted his fortune in riotous living. He squandered it all, and ended up in wanton destitution. In desperation, he took a job feeding hogs, and ended up in a pig pen. For a Jewish boy, that is about as low as he could go.

He began to think about his so-called friends, and also the consequences of his own indulgence. He was in as big a mess as anyone could imagine. Yet, in the middle of that pig pen, God spoke to his heart.

The young man had lost it all because he had wanted it all. He lost everything because he would not listen to his father. He ignored his advice and rejected his will. As a consequence the son lost his integrity and his dignity.

All the time he was in rebellion, the boy's father wanted only the best for him. In the same way, God only wants what is best for you. But you will never receive His best as long as you are wallowing in rebellion and self-pity.

This young man had big plans, but he left God out of his plans. It wasn't long until his dreams faded like a vapor. Countless business executives could testify that they thought they could have it all. But something went wrong and they lost it all. There are countless women who had a good husband, a wonderful family, a great job— everything seemed perfect. And then it all came crashing down!

No matter how bad your problems may be, God's grace is always greater! His mercy is deeper. His love is wider. His forgiveness is stronger than anything you could ever know. The Son of God who reached out to the prodigal son is still reaching out in love to you today.

Come to Yourself

In his most desperate hour, the young man found the solution to all his problems. We have no idea how long he remained in the pig pen. But the Bible says that he finally "came to himself" (Luke 15:17). My paraphrase would be that he "came to his senses."

The prodigal son saw himself for what he really was. He saw the consequences of his mistakes. But then, and only then, he realized who he really was—the child of his father.

Perhaps you, too, need to wake up and come to your senses. Perhaps it is time for you to come to the end of yourself and turn to your heavenly Father. Once you do, you'll be in a position where God can change you for the better.

Several years ago I was greeting the people as they left the church. A woman approached me and said, "Your sermon was excellent. Everything you said reminded me of a friend of mine. She really needed to hear that!"

Isn't that just like human nature? We can always see the flaw in someone else more quickly than we can see it in ourself. Yet our Lord reminded us that it is only when we come to personal repentance that we will ever unleash the power of His grace in our lives.

In Psalm 51, we see the beautiful picture of a broken man who had come to the end of himself and turned back to God. The psalm is written by David after his sin with Bathsheba. Prior to his confession and repentance, David testifies that he had lost the joy of his salvation. He even feared being cast out by God! Yet he is still God's child. But the guilt of his sin had robbed him of his joy and shaken his security.

In his prayer of repentance, David called upon God to wash away his sins, to cleanse his heart, and to blot out his transgressions. Then he asked God to create in him a clean heart, and to renew in him a right spirit. It is a prayer of repentance that leads to restoration of service.

David was called a man after God's heart (see 1 Sam. 13:14). Why? Because he, like the prodigal son, came to the end of himself. He came to his senses and he turned to God!

Remember Your Father's Resources

Home never seemed so good to the prodigal son as it did when he was starving in the pig pen. It was there that he remembered his father's great resources. Even his father's servants had plenty to eat.

A fresh awareness of your desperation can lead to an appreciation of your Father's resources. The prodigal son got up out of the pig pen, went home, and threw himself at his father's mercy.

Even in your most desperate hour, or your most despicable rebellion, you will have to come to the end of yourself. You will have to relinquish your rebellion and fall on your knees before the God whose resources are limitless.

God loves you with a love that goes beyond all human comprehension. Even when you have failed Him in the most serious way possible, He still loves you. He will not tolerate your sins, nor will He alleviate the consequences of your actions. But when you turn to Him, He will forgive you, cleanse you, and restore you to your rightful place of service in His kingdom.

Receive What God Has to Offer

The prodigal son came home, willing to work as a hired servant. He had come to the place that God could really use him. The Bible tells us the father saw him a "long way off." No doubt he had been searching for his son on the horizon day after day, hoping he would return. But on that certain day, he could hardly believe what he saw. It was his son—returned home!

The Bible tells us the father ran to meet the boy and embraced him and kissed him. He ordered his servants to place a ring on his finger, a coat on his back, and shoes on his feet. He brought him home to a banquet feast to welcome him back into his house and his fellowship.

When you and I have failed at the game of life, God stands ready to correct our mistakes. When we have fallen flat on our face, He stands ready to pick us up. Where we have wasted our human resources, He offers to us all the resources of His grace and power. There is no one who loves you like He loves you! There is no one willing to forgive you like He is willing to forgive you! There is no one willing to help you like He is willing to help you!

> *When you and I have failed at the game of life, God stands ready to correct our mistakes.*

Recently I had one of those terrible days. Everything seemed to go wrong. It reminded me of the infamous Murphy's Law: Whatever can go wrong, will go wrong. All day long, I felt that people were mean. I even received a letter with my name misspelled. I was so discouraged and frustrated by late afternoon that I felt like going home. Finally, I decided to leave my office and get some fresh air. As I walked out the door, a little boy skidded past me, being chased by his mother.

She caught the child, yanked him up, and dragged him over to where I was standing. Grabbing his face, she pointed it toward me and said, "Billy, if I've told you once, I've told you a thousand times, don't run in front of *nobody* again!"

It occurred to me she had just called me a *"nobody."* That was all I needed to let the bottom fall out of my day. Have you ever felt like that? That you really were insignificant and unimportant? Perhaps you think that nobody cares about you at all.

When we get to feeling like this, we're filled with self-pity and let our minds dwell on the negative factors of life, overlooking all the good things of life. Self-pity is the ultimate expression of self-centeredness. It is actually our way of admitting how selfish we are on the inside. Self-pity is the protest of self against the goodness of God. It is the refusal to be content with God's provisions for your life. It is a selfish demand that goes right to the very heart of life itself—a demand to have more, be more, and do more. In time, it is an attitude that leads to despair and depression.

The changes of life can add to our discouragement as well. Some people make the transition from childhood to adolescence very smoothly. For others it is the roughest ride imaginable. Some make the transition from adolescence to adulthood and seem to go on to success with relative ease. For others it is an incredible struggle that challenges the very essence and fiber of their being.

Changes are a part of life and they always will be. Challenges are also a part of life and they always will be. You and I can only be equal to the challenge when we are willing to understand that God is using these changes to grow our faith and mature our lives. He is preparing us for the future. By allowing the challenges and changes to come into our lives, God is motivating us to reach higher and farther than we ever have before. Such changes are not meant to defeat us or distress us. They are ultimately meant to demand the very best from within us.

We all stand on the precipice of change. Life is like hiking through the woods. There are times when the trail is smooth and easy. There are other times when it is rough and difficult. There are times when we must overcome obstacles. And there are times when the descent is relatively easy. At every juncture along the way, there are decisions to be made—decisions that will determine the course of our lives.

We are all pilgrims on the road of life. Life itself is a pilgrimage. It is a process of growth. There are no shortcuts to its destination. You can only get there by walking the road of life, though many obstacles may lie in your way. But it is in the process of learning to deal with the changes and challenges of life that we learn to deal with life itself. The problems are meant to make us better, not bitter.

> *Life itself is a pilgrimage. It is a process of growth. There are no shortcuts to its destination.*

The challenges and changes of life are the appointed opportunities to bring us to personal and spiritual maturity. Thus it is that we are pilgrims on the road of life. Never content with the temporal, we press on to the eternal.

I have always liked the way Robert Frost expressed it:

> I shall be telling you this with a sigh,
>> Somewhere ages and ages hence;
> Two lives diverged in a wood,
>> And I
> I took the one less traveled by,
>> And that has made all the difference![4]

The truth is that we all want to make a difference in this world. We want to do something better for ourselves, our family, and friends. That is because we are created in the image and likeness of God. We realize that life counts for something. And that is exactly what God has promised us. That regardless of the difficulties and challenges of life, God can use us to change the world for His glory!

Focus on the Future

1. What changes are you facing in your life, family, job, or church right now?

   _____

   _____

2. How are these changes affecting you and your family?

   You _____

   Spouse _____

   Children_____

   Extended Family _____

3. What areas is God trying to deal with you in your life through
   these challenges?

   _____

   _____

4. What progress are you making?

   _____

   _____

5. What progress do you need to make?

   _____

   _____

6. Are there any areas of failure that need to be resolved in your life?

   _____

   _____

7. What should you be doing about these?

   _____

   _____

   _____

   Remember, God can turn the worst of problems into the best of
results—if we let Him.

Part 2

Your Personal Plan for Future Success: Everything You Need to Know from A to Z

Things don't just happen by accident. They are the direct result of a chain reaction of events. One impacts the other until a *process* is set in motion. Eventually, that process flows into a series of processes which result in your future.

Right now, you are standing on the edge of a bright and wonderful future, if you will take responsibility for it. Once you do, you will be in a position to fully realize all that is available to you.

Some of us never realize our full potential because we are reluctant to take the steps of faith that will move us from the present into the future. The time has come for action. Step ahead by faith, knowing that God will guide your steps.

I have on the bookshelves of my study a set of *Encyclopedia Britannicas*. Within those numerous volumes are millions and millions of words that make up sentences, paragraphs, and articles of information. But think of it—each word, regardless of how many there are, is merely a combination of the twenty-six letters in the English alphabet, from A to Z.

Likewise, the future that lies before us will hold innumerable challenges for us all, but in each one that will come our way, I believe with a little effort and God's direction, we can find the combination to success. To help you get started right, let me suggest twenty-six steps to future successes that are as simple as A to Z.

Make sure you keep your priorities in order: God, family, others, self. Don't let good intentions get in your way. No excuses—it's time for action!

10

A—Accentuate the Positive

on't focus on the negatives. Look at the positives. Don't say, "It can't be done." Figure out how to do it! Don't complain. Move ahead. Set the pace. Make it happen to the glory of God.

If you were recruiting a small circle of management trainees to begin a new business, where would you look? If your future success totally depended upon the quality of your new recruits, you would certainly seek out the best, brightest, and sharpest people in your field of interest.

By contrast, Jesus called out fishermen, a tax collector, and a political outcast to build His church. They had no formal training. In fact, they had minimal personal ability. Most of them could not learn the lessons He tried to teach them without considerable difficulty.

Recently I stood on the shore of the Sea of Galilee, watching fishermen throwing their nets on the very waters where the disciples fished. I could not help but reflect on the fact that Jesus chose simple Galilean peasants to help Him change the world. He looked beyond outward appearances and saw the positive contribution each one of them could make to His ministry.

Remember the time Jesus fed the five thousand (John 6:1–15)? The disciples were focused on the problem, whereas Jesus was focused on the *solution*. They saw the limitations, but He saw the possibilities. They saw five loaves and two small fish. The Savior saw a banquet, with food left over!

Don't dwell on your difficulties. Minimize your frustrations. Maximize your possibilities. Focus on your future potential. Look up, not down. Look ahead, not back. Remember, your *attitude* is the key.

A couple had twin boys—one a confirmed pessimist and the other a habitual optimist. On their tenth birthday, their parents selected presents they hoped would balance out the boys' developing dispositions. For the pessimist, they wrapped up a bicycle, a remote control airplane, and a large box of chocolates. For the optimist, they arranged to have a local landscaper dump a massive pile of manure on the driveway.

In the morning, the parents were shocked to see the pessimist crying and sobbing. "Are you trying to kill me?" he shrieked. "I'll probably wreck the bicycles, crash the airplane, and rot my teeth out with the candy!" In the meantime, they heard shouts of joy from out on the driveway, where the optimist was busily digging in the pile of manure.

"Why are you so happy?" they asked.

"I just know there has to be a pony underneath all this mess!" he exclaimed.

Whatever life dumps your way, accentuate the positive.

11

B—Believe It Can Happen

There is a story told in Acts 12 that hits close to home for all of us. The apostle Peter had been imprisoned for preaching the gospel. He was placed in maximum security, chained between two soldiers, and guarded by four squads. So the early church gathered to pray for his release. But their earnest prayer meeting at Mary's home was interrupted by a knock at the gate. It was Peter himself! He had been released miraculously by an angel. When he came to the gate of their yard, Rhoda went out to meet him. Surprised and excited, she ran into the house to announce Peter's arrival—only to discover that no one believed her! We too often pray for something, all the time thinking it will never really come to pass.

During the last century, George Mueller, who devoted a large part of his life to caring for orphans, was known for his *faith* in answered prayer. Mueller even made a habit of praying for the daily needs of himself and his orphans. He also prayed every day for more than fifty years for the salvation of two friends by name.

"Why don't you give up?" another friend suggested. "If God wanted to convert them, He would have done it by now."

Mueller simply turned to Galatians 6:9: "Let us not be weary in well-doing: for in due season we shall reap, if we faint not."

"It's God's duty to harvest," George replied. "It is mine to not give up!"

One man was converted a month before Mueller died, and the other was saved at his funeral![1]

We can't presume to know the will of God for everybody else. But we can seek to know it for ourselves. When we have placed all our hope in God, we should not be surprised when He answers our prayers. Don't be shocked at the power of faith. Jesus once said, "According to your faith be it unto you" (Matt. 9:29).

If God moves in proportion to your faith, how significant will His moving be in your life?

12

C–Commit Yourself Totally

Half-hearted faith never gets the job done. If you really want to impact the future, commit yourself totally to it today. You can't learn to roller-skate sitting on the couch. At some point you must make a commitment to get started—even if it costs you something.

There is a humorous story told about a conversation between a pig and a chicken.

"The farmer is so nice to us," the chicken suggested, "let's make breakfast for him tomorrow.

"Fine," said the pig. "What did you have in mind?"

"How about ham and eggs?" suggested the chicken.

"Forget it!" protested the pig. "For you, that's only a gift. But for me it's total commitment!"

Unfortunately, that's what it usually takes to get the job done. We can't put forth half-hearted effort and get whole-hog results!

The prophet Elijah learned this lesson on Mount Carmel. He confronted 850 false prophets and Ahab, the king of Israel, with the challenge: "The God that answereth by fire, let him be God" (1 Kings 18:24).

Elijah put himself at great disadvantage:

• He was outnumbered 850–1.

- He met the Baal prophets on their "home court" at Mount Carmel.
- He chose a sign associated with their god (e.g., lightning).
- He let them choose their sacrifice first.
- He let them go first and call upon Baal.

Elijah left no margin of error—no easy way of escape. He stood surrounded by the exhausted prophets of Baal, an angry King Ahab, and a skeptical crowd of spectators. His life, his ministry, and his entire future was at stake—totally committed to God.

If you travel to Mount Carmel today, you will find a beautiful monument commemorating Elijah's victory. The white marble statue stands glistening in the sun as a reminder of the success of the prophet's total commitment to God.

Such commitment is vital to every area of our lives. "Let's try it and see if it works," won't do in most situations. In fact, it is the very force of your commitment that enables you to weather the storms of life.

Part of the scenic beauty of England are the many stone walls that dot the countryside. Over the generations, the local folks have made an art form out of building these walls, fitting natural stones together to divine the fields and pastures.

One Englishman tells of the challenge of climbing over those walls. "Whenever we came upon one that seemed insurmountable," he explained, "we just threw our caps over it, leaving us no alternative but to go fetch them!"

Perhaps you've grown stale with indecision. Maybe it's time to throw your cap over the wall. Make the decision. Commit yourself totally. Now's the time for action!

13

D–Decide to Make a Difference

I once asked a group of senior citizens what regrets, if any, they had about life. "I wish I had risked more," several said. "I wish I had invested my energy in things that would outlive me," others added.

Leaving a legacy is vital to a successful life. At the end of the road, no one is really content to have lived for himself alone. We need to be able to look back and see that we really did make a difference in this world.

Personal Prerogative. Anyone making a decision must assume the responsibilities of that decision. We can't just sit back, do nothing, and hope things will get better. We must act decisively. God is proactive. And so must we be. He took the initiative to reach out to us. Now, we must take the initiative to reach out to others.

Positive Plan. You will never reach your destination if you aren't willing to get going in the right direction. During the attack on Pearl Harbor at the start of World War II, a young naval officer found himself the senior commander left on one of the ships. "Can you take the ship out to sea?" radioed Harbor Control. "Can do!" came the officer's two-word reply. It became the rallying cry for the entire U.S. Navy.[1]

Purposeful Potential. God has promised to empower us to fulfill His purposes in our lives. You don't have to do it alone. God is at work in your life. Let Him have control. Let Him reveal His will and intentions for your life. The Bible promises, "I can do all things through Christ which strengtheneth me" (Phil. 4:13).

Naturalist Loren Eiseley relates a moving story about his visit to the beach at Costabel. Walking along the seashore early one morning, Eiseley noticed a young man in the distance dancing along the water's edge. As he drew closer, he realized the young man was picking up starfish stranded by the tide and flipping them back to safety in the ocean.

At first, the naturalist was disturbed by this interruption in the natural order. He told the young "star thrower" that there were miles of beach and thousands of stranded starfish.

"You can't possibly make a difference!" Eiseley shouted at him.

Without a word, the young man picked up another starfish and threw it well out into the waves. Looking directly into the naturalist's eyes, the boy said, "It made a difference for that one!"[2]

14

E—Eliminate the Negative

Negative attitudes are like heavy weights upon our hearts. They slow us down and keep us from making progress. That's why serious runners don't carry a lot with them. Weight is a hindrance. That's also why we can't run the race of life weighed down with negatives.

I once heard a humorous story about a lady who went to see her doctor with some pretty serious symptoms.

"Madame, your tests reveal that you have an acute case of rabies!" her doctor told her. "This is serious!" he added. "You ought to put your affairs in order."

"All right then, give me a pen and some paper," she demanded.

"You can wait until you consult your lawyer," the doctor suggested.

"I'm not writing a will," she replied. "This is a list of people I want to bite!"

Eliminating the negatives is like getting the weeds out of your garden. Once the weeds are gone, everything else will grow better on its own. Otherwise, your yard can turn into a jungle!

Unfortunately, there are some people who are so full of negatives that they have no room for any positives. Their lives are filled with bitterness and frustration. Like Georgia kudzu, everything is overgrown—and choked by weeds.

Notice the difference your attitude can make:

NEGATIVE	POSITIVE
We've never done it before.	We have the opportunity to be first.
This will never work.	Let's give it a try.
We've already tried it	We can learn from our mistakes.
It's not my responsibility.	I'll take the responsibility.
We don't need to change.	There's always room for improvement.

For some of us, the negatives are attitudes. But for others, they are habits. "Besetting sins," the Bible calls them. Oh, they don't have to be large, just pesky. They don't even have to be grossly immoral, just naggingly persistent.

This may be a good time to take a spiritual inventory of your life. Ask God to reveal the negatives in your life: attitudes, habits, fears, failure. Make a mental list. Then ask yourself what you need to do with each one. Chances are God will tell you to get rid of it. Why not start right now!

15

F—Find Your Options

Some people never make any progress because they remain stuck in a rut. Too satisfied with their current situation, they fail to look at all of their options for making improvement. Whenever you fail to check out your options, you may miss your greatest opportunities.

I remember hearing about a business meeting which became gridlocked over one man's dissenting vote. While the issue was rather trivial, it did require unanimous approval. The meeting dragged on, and neither logic nor reason would prevail. Finally, one of the board members asked to meet with the dissenting person. They stepped out into the hallway, and the board member dragged him over to the window and told him he was going to throw him out the window if he didn't change his vote.

In a few moments the two men returned to the room and the dissenter changed his vote, giving unanimous approval for the board action. When someone approached him later and asked him why he finally changed his vote, the man explained, "I changed my mind when the other fellow took the time to explain my options!"

There is an interesting story in the Bible about four lepers who were running out of options. The Syrian army had surrounded the city of Samaria and was starving them into surrender. The lepers sought safety in the city, but were locked out by the inhabitants. As they sat before the locked gate, they realized they were trapped between the approaching Syrians and the starving Samaritans. All of their options looked bleak, when one of them spoke up and suggested they should throw themselves on the mercy of the enemy. That night they left the gate and made their way out to the camp of the Syrians only to discover that the enemy had panicked and run back to Syria, leaving all their possessions behind (see 2 Kings 7:3–5).

When the lepers realized what had happened, they ran from tent to tent, hoarding up all the goods they could find. Their spirit of consumerism was a lot like the bumper sticker we often read today: "He who dies with the most toys wins!"

The lepers finally came under conviction and decided to go back and tell the people in the city what good fortune had befallen them. Their options had turned to their own success and now they were willing to share that success with others.

This story reminds us there are three kinds of people in life:

Sitters—For several days the lepers just sat in front of the gate until they finally looked at each other and said, "Why should we sit here until we die?" Too many people are just like that. They sit through life like a giant "couch potato" and never really get involved. They spend all their time sitting around complaining about their problems instead of getting up and doing something about it.

Getters—Once the others decided to act, they got greedy. They ran from tent to tent hoarding everything they could get their hands on. Unfortunately, this is all too often the attitude of people today. They are willing to get involved, but only for their own benefit. Their major interest in life is "what's in it for me?" Those who focus on getting, instead of giving, will never be satisfied. Because the more you get, the more you want. And the more you have, the less satisfied you become.

Givers—It was only when the lepers realized that "this is the day of good tidings" that they were willing to go share the good news with others. Once we get our eyes off ourselves and onto the needs of others, we put ourselves into the position to realize it is "more blessed to give than receive." There is a world of need at your doorstep. When we learn to give whatever is necessary to meet others' needs, people will line up to receive the gift of ministry that we are willing to share with them. There are always more options than we think. Get your eyes off yourself, and start looking for places to help.

16

G—Give It All You Have

There is something about the intensity of athletic competition that captures our attention. Here in Atlanta everyone is focused on the Centennial Olympic Games. Roads are being widened, bridges constructed, and buildings remodeled in preparation for the "Event of the Century." A gigantic Olympic stadium is taking shape downtown, and preparations are being made at various sites all around the city.

We all get excited about the intensity of great athletic events. The same was true in Bible times. The apostle Paul often referred to athletic events in his writings. In one passage, he actually makes the statement, "Forgetting those things which are behind, and reaching forth unto those things which are before, I press toward the mark for the prize of the high calling of God in Christ Jesus" (Phil. 3:13–14).

Pressing toward the finish line is not the only endeavor which requires maximum effort. Every area of our lives makes similar requirements of us. Parenting may push you to the very limits of human exhaustion. Your business involvement may stretch your heart, mind, and soul. Your family and church involvement may require discipline and determination. A Moravian missionary once put it like this: "We have a short time to win our victories, but all eternity to celebrate them."

Giving it all you have requires cooperation. All of us at one time or other have been procrastinators. How many times have you put off even the minimal preparation that was necessary in order to get the job done? As the deadline came bearing down upon you, you continued to delay taking action. Why do we do that? Because we realize the effort that's going to have to be made, and the price that will have to be paid to get the job done.

Giving it all you have means having a total focus. Maximum effort does not usually compensate for poor preparation and lack of planning. Unfortunately, too many of us are so distracted by the world, that we fail to focus on that which is really important. Giving it all you have will mean forsaking what is unimportant, focusing on what is essential, and doing what is necessary. You can't have a great marriage by simply wishing it so. It will take work, effort, discipline, and self-denial to make it happen. You will never be successful in business without establishing and focusing on the goal of fruitfulness and success. And you'll never have the one without the other.

Giving it all you have begins by being willing to give yourself—totally and completely. Unconditional surrender to the will and purpose of God. These are the ingredients that ultimately make for real success. This is what it will take to hear the Savior say, "Well done, good and faithful servant."

17

H—Hope for the Best

It is not an accident that our television ministry is called *There's Hope!* It was founded on the basic premise that God is in the business of giving hope to believers and hope to seekers.

A young mother once wrote me and shared how she had abandoned all hope. A failed marriage, estranged children, and the loss of a job had driven her to the point of suicide. She sat alone one Sunday morning, contemplating how she would take her own life, when our broadcast came on her television set. The very words of our program name—*There's Hope!*—captured her attention. She decided to postpone her suicide and began attending our church to see if there really was hope for her in the midst of her difficult circumstances.

It wasn't long until she found that Jesus Christ was a Savior who would love her, forgive her, and restore her in every way. She gave her life to Him and began to grow in her spiritual walk with God. Today she is a regular and active member of our church. She is involved in several of our outreach ministries, sharing her faith with others. The same God who met her needs can meet yours. He can intervene in your life and give you the hope you need to face your future as well.

One of the young couples in our church came to me with a frantic appeal for help. The woman had been diagnosed with a terminal brain tumor. Her doctor told her she only had six months to live. She had collapsed on the kitchen floor and was rushed to the hospital where the diagnosis was made. But instead of giving up hope, they came to my office for prayer and counsel.

I reminded them that where there is life, there's hope! The woman went on to have a very delicate surgery with only a marginal chance of success. We prayed for her healing that day in my office, and then called our church to special prayer for her as well. Healing may not always be in the plan of God, but in this case it was. Even the unbelieving surgeon called the operation a "miracle." Through it all, the young couple never lost hope. They believed that God had a plan and that they could trust Him to fulfill His plan in every detail of their lives.

It is in the times of trials and crises that God speaks most loudly. When difficulties come we can either trust Him with hope and confidence or collapse in fear and depression. The strongest testimonies I have ever seen have been forged in the furnace of bitter trials, tempered by the flames of crisis. When the circumstances of life turn sour, people need to learn to turn to the Savior.

When the going gets tough, God gets tougher! The power and sufficiency of His grace is enough to help us through any difficulty in life. Even in the worst of times, God can do the best of things. When all else fails, hope for the best, expect to be blessed, and trust God to see you through.

18

I–Initiate a Plan of Action

Actions reflect beliefs. We do what we do because we believe what we believe. If we were convinced that we could climb the highest mountain, we would make an attempt to do so. However, none of us ever come close to reaching our goals, because we do not really believe that they are attainable.

There is an interesting story told in the Old Testament about the Moabite rebellion against Israel and Judah (see 2 Kings 3:9–20). During the conflict, the armies of Israel and Judah marched seven days through the wilderness. Their water ran out by the end of the week. Soldiers can survive without food, but their ability to fight in the desert climate without water is next to impossible. Having consulted with the prophet Elisha, the kings ordered them to started digging ditches.

Now if I had been a soldier in Israel's army, I might have questioned my orders. Sometimes the directions of leadership make little sense to those who are in a position of followship. The order to dig ditches was probably considered completely unreasonable.

Have you ever dug a ditch on a hot day? If you have you remember how unbearably hot it is and how profusely you perspire. Most of us could not get through such an ordeal without an adequate supply of water. Unfortunately, the soldiers of Israel and Judah had no such relief. Given the undesirable orders they had received, they were certainly put in a place of attempting to do the impossible. Think of the possible negative reactions:

Distraction. "I'll get the shovels." Some people will do anything except the job at hand. They even might gather the equipment, but don't ask them to do the digging!

Discouragement. "We'll never be able to do it." Whenever work is hard, and progress is slow, it is easy for people to get discouraged. It is also easy to focus on the negatives, rather than the positives. I'm convinced that to get the job done, we often have to overcome our initial discouragement.

Disbelief. "Are you crazy?" I'm sure some of the Israelites were shocked at some of their leaders' requests. Whenever we don't believe something can happen, we won't put forth the effort to make it happen. We have to overcome our initial disbelief in order to accomplish the impossible for the glory of God.

Defeat. "It can't be done!" Some people are self-ordained experts on how nothing can be done. They infiltrate our churches, boards, and circles of confidence. Their battle cry is, "Don't even try it because it will fail!" A World War I field marshall once said, "No army is defeated until they believe they are defeated."

You can't succeed without a plan of action. As incredible as it sounds, after the Israelites had dug the ditches, a rainstorm came and filled their "wells." There are many times in our lives that we must step out by faith, initiate a plan of action, and trust God with the results. This is no time to sit around doing nothing. The time has come to get up and get going to the glory of God!

19

J—Jump in All the Way

Have you ever watched children playing in a swimming hole? Some walk up to the water's edge and stick in their toes to test the water. Others just run full speed ahead and jump right on in. When I was a boy we decided to go swimming in a little pond. The sky was blue, the sun was bright, and the air seemed warm and balmy. While the other kids stood on the edge of the pond with their toes pointed forward toward the water's edge, I ran headlong and jumped in like a rolled up cannonball. The air was warm, but the water was freezing! The shock of the cold took my breath away. But once I was in the water, I decided to make the best of it and went swimming anyway. Everybody else made a decision to go swimming, but I made a total commitment!

Sometimes it's that kind of commitment that is necessary for us to act by faith and activate the power of God in our lives. When the prophet Elisha requested that Naaman, the leper from Syria, dip himself seven times in the Jordan River, the Syrian commander objected strenuously. Elisha reminded him it was his act of faith and obedience that would activate the power of God on his behalf (2 Kings 5:10–14). Naaman had even suggested that he use the rivers of Damascus back home. But Elisha reminded him that it was just as inadequate to jump into their own river as it was not to jump at all.

Despite all his excuses and objections, Naaman finally did what the prophet requested him to do. He dipped seven times into the Jordan

River. To the general's credit, he did indeed jump in all the way, and came up healed of his leprosy. Total commitment made all the difference in his life, and it can make all the difference in yours. When God's will is clear, jump in all the way!

20

K–Knock on Every Door

Building a church is a lot like building a business. Every Tuesday night, we send out hundreds of people to knock on doors all over Atlanta. The more doors we knock on, the more visitors we have attending our services the following week. I'm not suggesting that this always works like a mathematical formula, but often it does. Churches that are not willing to reach out to their community will find that their community does not reach out to them.

One evening when the weather was particularly unpleasant, we had knocked on several doors where no one was home. There was a great temptation to give up for the evening and return to the church. Instead, I decided to try one more prospect. A shaggy, long-haired, young man, with multiple earrings and tattooed biceps, came to the door. As I began my conversation, he interrupted me and gruffly demanded, "Do you know how to become a Christian?"

Shocked by his question, I responded that I certainly did! I shared the gospel with him and asked him if he would be willing to give his life to Jesus Christ. He told me he had attended church two days before with a friend, and during the public invitation he had resisted the call of God for his life. For the next two days he had been praying, "Lord, give me another chance."

There is no telling how many people are waiting for us to reach out to them, if we are just willing to knock on their door one more time. Even in the area of our own lives, it is important that we learn to explore all our options, knock on every door, and try every opportunity before we ever give up on the plan and will of God.

No one who has visited the Lincoln Memorial can leave without a lasting impression of that great man who made such a mark on history. When we think of Abraham Lincoln, we immediately associate him with the presidency. History records that he had two failed businesses, he lost eight elections, and had a nervous breakdown, all before finally being elected President of the United States. Abraham Lincoln obviously knew the importance of knocking on every door.

Why do we quit knocking? Mostly because we get discouraged! We start believing that we cannot succeed, so we stop trying. Our pride gets hurt, and we focus on our rejection instead of our resources. We get our eyes off of God and onto ourselves.

But the bottom line is this: Don't give up on the power of God. Keep believing! Keep on knocking! And one day the door of opportunity will stand open wide.

21

L—Live Up to Your Potential

You are an ambassador for Jesus Christ. You have been commissioned and sent on the Father's business. And if you really understand your position in Christ, you will realize the necessity of living up to your potential in Christ.

The Scripture says in Romans 8:37, "In all these things we are more than conquerors through him that loved us." An ambassador's power comes from his position. His power is symbolic of the nation he represents. We, too, as believers, are called upon to be representatives of Christ in the world. If you have ever driven along Embassy Row in Washington, D.C., you realize the unusual entity that is represented by each embassy. A small piece of foreign territory is actually sovereignly held by the particular nations represented. At the same time, we believers need to realize that we represent a little bit of heaven everywhere we go.

An ambassador for Christ stands "in Christ's stead." We represent Jesus Christ, bearing His name, and bearing the reproach of the cross to a world that is desperately wanting to know whether Christianity is for real. We are commissioned as His ambassadors to bring people into the kingdom of Christ. Just as the ambassadors of a nation are called upon to represent that nation and to reconcile its enemies to peace, so we, too, must carry the message of Christ even to those who are our enemies.

Knowing God is one thing, but knowing who you are in Christ is another. Some people come to church every week, knowing that they believe in God. They may even have a personal relationship with Jesus Christ. But all too often they fail to realize who they are in Christ. Through Him we share all the authority and blessings of the person of Christ Himself. There are no second-class citizens in the kingdom of heaven. Those who have born by faith into the family of God have an equal status before the Father. Sometimes it is important to remind ourselves of who we really are and what our responsibility really is.

22

M—Motivate Others

My father once told me, "Son, the only way for you to do the work of ten men is to motivate ten men to help you." Getting the job done in any area of life will often involve motivating others to help us. Remember, even the Lone Ranger had a partner! Most of us are familiar with David's famous victory over Goliath. But we often forget that it was that victory that motivated Saul's army to pursue the enemy and overcome them.

Motivation requires preparation. We motivate best by our own personal example. David approached the giant and overcame him. It was certainly an indication of the power of God in response to the faith of His people.

Motivation also requires consistency. David approached the giant in the same manner in which he had approached life's other challenges—in the power of God. David later became a great leader because he was a great follower. Willing to obey, God placed him in a position to lead others.

That's why it's so important for parents to back up their words with their actions. Our lives must be consistent with our requests. You can't yell at your children for yelling with each other without being inconsistent. You can't expect them to do what you assign and not do what you're doing.

Motivation also requires faith in your cause. You have to believe in what you're doing in order to motivate others to follow you. David's faith in God was so overwhelming that it overpowered everyone—including his brothers, King Saul, Goliath, and the whole Philistine army! There is no doubt that he was totally surrendered to God's will and purpose for his life.

William Carey, the famous English Baptist missionary, labored for seven years in India before he won his first convert—his own house-boy! But Carey never gave up because he believed in the cause of God to which he had surrendered himself so valiantly. In time, Carey was able to train others to help him. He even set up a business to help support his missionary enterprise. Before long, he had a self-supporting mission which reached thousands of Indians with the gospel of Christ. But he didn't do it alone. He learned how to motivate others, including the Indians themselves, to help him.

Jesus spent three years training twelve disciples. Though one of them was a traitor, and though all of them failed Him at times, they eventually turned their world upside down!

Even today, our Lord can use us to "make disciples" of others and equip them to evangelize the world, teach the believers, and build up the church. If God does not work without human instrumentality, then neither should we! The more you can get others involved in sharing your vision, fulfilling your burden, and extending your ministry, the more effectively you can get the job done to the glory of God.

23

N–Never Give Up

Winston Churchill was asked to address his alma mater during the dark days of World War II. As he approached the podium, he said, "Never give up! Never give up! Never, never, never give up!"[1] Then he sat down. It was one of the shortest, most memorable commencement addresses ever given. The speech reflected the spirit and determination of England's greatest prime minister.

In the early days of the war, on June 4, 1940, after the British evacuation at Dunkirk, Winston Churchill addressed the British Parliament. He closed his dramatic speech with these challenging words: "We shall go to the end, we shall fight in France, we shall fight on the seas and the oceans, we shall fight with growing confidence, and growing strength, we shall defend our home, whatever the cost shall be. We shall fight on the beaches, we shall fight on the landing grounds, we shall fight in the fields and the streets, we shall fight in the hills; we shall never surrender!"[2]

One does not have to be an expert in European history to realize that the determination of Winston Churchill was one of the key factors in Britain's success in World War II. He personally determined, by the grace of God and the grit of the British people, to win the war. Because he would not give up, the people of Britain did not give up.

The Bible is filled with stories of determined faith. One that has always moved my heart is that of blind Bartimaeus. He sat begging on the highway outside Jericho. When he heard Jesus was passing by, he cried out, saying: "Jesus, thou son of David, have mercy on me" (Mark 10:47). When the crowd rebuked him and told him to be quiet, he cried all the more until he got the Savior's attention.

It is interesting to observe that Bartimaeus could not see, but he could hear. He understood who it was that was passing by. He could not see, but he could pray. He cried out to the Son of God for help. He could not see, but he could speak. The more he spoke, the more the Savior listened.

Bartimaeus was healed because he would not take no for an answer. He would not give up on his desperate condition. He kept crying out until he got the Savior's attention and found the solution for which he sought.

Chuck Colson tells a powerful story of the determination of Alexander Solzhenitsyn, a prisoner in a Soviet gulag. Despite long days of hard labor and slave starvation, Solzhenitsyn determined to fight on within his own spirit. One day the hopelessness became too much to bear. Feeling there was no reason to fight any longer, he laid down his shovel and slumped onto his work bench. He knew that any moment the guard would order him to stand up and bludgeon him to death if he did not respond.

As he sat there, feeling hopeless, he noticed an old man with a wrinkled and expressionless face stooping over near him. The man drew a stick through the sand at Solzhenitsyn's feet, deliberately tracing the sign of the cross. As he stared at the rough outline, Alexander's entire perspective changed. Solzhenitsyn realized that the cross symbolized the fact that anything is possible by the power of God. He stood slowly, picked up his shovel, and went back to work.

Colson comments, "Such is the power God's truth affords one man willing to stand against seemingly hopeless odds. Such is the power of the cross."[3]

24

O—Overcome the Obstacles

Military engineers throughout history have provided us with amazing stories of their ability to overcome insurmountable obstacles. Their attitude is summed up by the construction battalions of the U.S. Navy, the SeaBees. Their motto is, "Can do!" Throughout history there have been several examples of incredible feats of overcoming unbelievable obstacles.

Babylon. Herodotus records that the walled defenses of Babylon rose nearly 200 feet with a beveled double wall system around the entire city. The walls were 14 miles square and 187 feet thick at the base. Without a doubt, the walls of Babylon were the mightiest defensive work in ancient history. When King Cyrus of the Medeo-Persian alliance and his General Gobryas confronted the city, the obstacles seemed too great. Yet, on October 16, 539 B.C., Cyrus entered Babylon as the victor. Rather than trying to bridge the mighty walls directly, his engineers diverted the Euphrates River, which flowed under its walls, allowing his soldiers to march under the walls by night to capture the city.

Tyre. In the days of Alexander the Great, Tyre was known as the unconquerable city. Set on an island, surrounded by sea, Tyre enjoyed autonomy and would not surrender to Alexander's army. In 332 B.C., Alexander laid siege and began construction of a massive causeway stretching from the mainland toward the island. After seven months of labor, the massive dirt and stone pier was completed, allowing the

Macedonian armies to march to Tyre on dry ground and take the city without losing a man.

Masada. The desert fortress near the Dead Sea was the last outpost of the Jewish rebellion against the Roman Empire. Built originally by Herod the Great, Masada was constructed to withstand any siege. Towering four hundred meters above the Western Shore of the Dead Sea, Masada was unapproachable on two sides, and only by a narrow winding path from the East. Great cisterns were built inside the mountain fortress to hold enough water and grain to withstand a siege of any length.

The Roman general Silva surveyed Masada in the winter of A.D. 72. He realized the fortress was virtually impregnable. In an incredible feat of engineering, his Tenth Legionaires endeavored for seven months to build a dirt ramp upon the side of the mountain upon which they rolled a battering ram to bridge the walls of the fortress. When the Romans finally entered Masada, they found the entire population of 960 men, women, and children had committed suicide rather than surrender. To this day, Masada is an Israeli symbol of independence and determination.

To most of us, the obstacles of life are much more personal: lack of education, physical limitations, lack of opportunities, or resources. There is a young man in our church whose name is Kevin. Kevin is in a wheelchair, and he struggles with even the simplest of movements. You have to concentrate to understand what he is saying, because of the limitations of his speech. But Kevin does not allow the obstacles of his physical limitations to prevent him from living a successful life. He has a circle of friends in our Single Adult Ministry who support him and bring him to church. He rarely misses a service. He has trained his mind in computers and has a full-time job as a writer for technical manuals. Although Kevin struggles with his spoken words, he expresses himself eloquently on the computer bulletin board via modem. Without a doubt, he has learned to overcome some of the greatest obstacles of life. The smile on his face, the song in his heart, reveal in his life a wonder to behold.

You and I have few viable excuses for failing to overcome life's obstacles. We have a God who is greater than any of the problems of life. We have the power of His indwelling Holy Spirit within our lives. We have the truth of His Word to guide us. We have the family of God to encourage us. With all those things working for us, we surely must say triumphantly, "If God be for us, who can be against us!"

25

P–Practice Makes Perfect

A tourist once asked a passing maestro, "How do you get to Carnegie Hall?"

"Practice! Practice! Practice!" was the conductor's reply.

Anyone who has ever played golf realizes that the real masters of the game did not achieve what they did by accident. Golf, like music, takes an incredible amount of practice. The slightest inconsistency in one's swing can result in slicing the ball into the woods, creeks, or sand traps. Playing golf isn't easy. But with plenty of practice it can be a challenging and fulfilling activity.

Most of us watch professional athletes perform great feats of accomplishment and we just sit there thinking it really is fairly easy. We are also accustomed to the work of a superstar like Michael Jordan in that we come to take such work for granted. But the slightest break in rhythm, or missing of one's timing by a split-second can result in disaster.

It has often been said that only practice "makes perfect." There is something about the discipline and consistency of practice that is absolutely essential in every area of life.

Living the Christian life and sharing your faith effectively doesn't happen by accident either. The Campus Crusade manual makes this statement: "This process cannot be confined to classroom lectures. It will necessarily branch out into practical situations."[1] The manual goes on to explain that a half-hearted, let-the-chips-fall-where-they-may attitude does not work effectively in reaching people for Christ. Nothing less than rigorous and effective evangelistic training is adequate in equipping workers for the harvest.

We can observe the difference between our Lord's example as an *evangelist* and His example as a *trainer of evangelists*. One writer has observed that Jesus established with His training guidelines: total foresight of what to say; to whom they should speak and not speak; what to take with them; with whom to stay; how to be supported; what to do in case of objection; and what to expect in terms of opposition.[2]

Learning what to say provides tracks on which to run. Such instruction gives a person confidence to handle a wide range of opportunities. But practical experience, or on-the-job training, allows us to become experienced in dealing with people in all situations.

One of the ladies in our church was being trained in the Evangelism Explosion approach to personal witnessing. While she was sitting around the dinner table with her extended family at Thanksgiving, she heard a nephew tell about a near-death experience he had recently on an oil derrick. After listening to his conversation about his near tragedy, she asked, "Eric, have you come to the place in your spiritual life where you know for certain that if you had died on that oil platform, you would now be in heaven?" His resulting answer gave her the opportunity to share Christ with her extended family, and four people committed their lives to the Savior that day!

Thus, practice makes perfect in music, sports, and in sharing your faith. Instead of waiting for opportunities to happen, why not practice, practice, practice! The more you practice living out your faith and sharing it with others, the more effective you will become as a witness for the Savior. The more you share, the more results you will experience.

26

Q–Quit Making Excuses

Excuses are rampant. I recently read an explanation of why people feel so overworked. The clever article in a church newsletter explained that of the 200 million people in the United States, 84 million were over the age of 65, leaving only 116 million to do the work. Those under 20 years of age totaled another 75 million, leaving only 41 million people to do the work. Of these, 22 million are employed by the government, leaving only 19 million to do the work. Deduct 15 million state and city employees, and 4 million people in hospitals and mental institutions, and there are only a handful of people left to do the work. By the time the clever article finished, there were only two people left to do any work at all! The one came to the other and said, "There's no one left but you and me. And I'm getting tired of doing everything myself!"

The problem really isn't that bad in reality. But it often seems that way. More often than not, we run into people who would rather make excuses than get the job done. Let me encourage you to stop making excuses and start moving ahead. Excuses are nothing more than lies wrapped in the ribbons of rationalization. There is no excuse for failing to take responsibility and tackle the jobs that lie in our path. Too many husbands excuse their failure as a spouse or a parent because they claim they're tired. But they will turn right around and go hunting for hours! They will sit outside in terrible weather at a football game and scream to the top of their lungs, then claim that they can't stand crowds and excuse themselves from attending church. People will spend money to eat out in restaurants, go to shopping malls, and invest in all kinds of hobbies, but claim they don't have any money.

Life is filled with excuses. In the ministry, you hear them all:

- "It's the preacher's job."
- "It's not my gift."
- "I'm too shy."
- "I'm too busy."
- "This isn't a good time."
- "Someone else could do it better."

Even when it comes to the issue of a person's eternal salvation, many will begin to make excuses. Someone has also described an excuse as the "skin of a reason stuffed with a lie." Yet it is interesting that at the last judgment the Father says, people will be "without excuse" (Rom. 1:29). Could that be you? Are you hiding behind your excuses? Quit making excuses! Be responsible! If you don't, you have no one to blame but yourself!

27

R—Reach for the Ultimate

On August 8, 1970, Larry Doumis pulled a sixty-five-pound lake trout out of the Great Bear Lake in Canada. Can you imagine bringing that whopper home to clean? Some people spend their entire life fishing for the big one and never get it. Others keep reaching for the ultimate goal, believing that one day it will be theirs.

Jesus challenged His disciples, who were mostly fishermen by trade, to get involved in the ultimate. He told them He wanted to make them "fishers of men" (Matt. 4:19). He challenged them beyond their human capacity to perform. He challenged them with a vision that was beyond themselves. In fact, He challenged them to become what indeed they were not!

God is still in the business of challenging people. Don't settle for second best. Remember who you are in Christ, and what it is to which you have been called by Him.

The key to success in any area of life is *desire.* If you want something desperately enough, you will do whatever is necessary to get it. Professional athletes who aspire to greatness have found the only way to achieve it is by self-sacrifice and personal discipline. Those who develop a passion for art, literature, and drama have found that the only way to success is that of total determination.

Henry Kimball was a shoe salesman in Boston. He was also a Sunday School teacher with a heart for people. One day he shared his faith in Christ with a young man named Dwight L. Moody. In time, Moody's life was dramatically changed by the power of God. He became one of America's greatest evangelists, and, through his preaching, F. B. Meyer came to Christ. In turn, Meyer led Wilbur Chapman to Christ. Later, a professional baseball player, Billy Sunday, heard Chapman preach and gave his life to Christ. Still later, Mordecai Hamm accepted the Lord at one of Billy Sunday's revivals. In time, Mordecai Hamm preached in a tent revival in North Carolina, and a young man named Billy Graham responded to his invitation.

Millions of people have been won to Christ because a shoe clerk was faithful to share the message of Christ. Though his mission task may have seemed menial, he was really involved in that which is the ultimate priority to the heart of God—sharing the message of the gospel with others. Don't be content with less than the best. Don't think that what you are doing in your day-to-day life is insignificant. That which is done by faith becomes the best and produces eternal results.

28

S–Start Each Day with Prayer

P rayer is a marvelous means of reaching the heavens! The prayer of James Moffat was for God to send missionaries to Africa. While speaking at a conference in Glasgow, he described the view from the southern tip of Africa where he ministers. "As I look toward Africa, I see the smoke of one thousand villages who have not heard the name of Jesus." Such a challenge seized the heart of young David Livingston. Despite the protestations of his contemporaries, Livingston went to Africa and was lost from public view for several years.

When he was finally found by Henry M. Stanley, a reporter for the *London Times* ("Dr. Livingston, I presume"), he was near death in Ujiji, West Africa. Livingston had given the medicine needed to treat his own malaria to other people and was a few days away from exhausting his supply.

One of the enduring memorials that we have to Livingston are three lines of prayer found in his journal:

"Send me anywhere, only go with me." A Christian should begin each day reporting for duty. We need to be reminded that we are soldiers in the army of God and don't control our own agenda. We should be ready to go where God directs. I heard of a new member sitting in church, listening to the preacher speak about heaven. Abruptly the preacher asked the congregation, "How many of you want to go to

heaven?" Every hand went up except for the new member. After the service, the pastor quietly sought him out, "Don't you want to go to heaven?" "Certainly I want to go," said the new member, "I just thought you were trying to get up a load tonight!"

"Lay any burden on me, only sustain me." Jesus calls each of us to be servants, literally slaves. What makes a servant significant? Possessions and wealth ultimately mean little to a servant, because everything he has is controlled by the master. What makes a servant significant is his master! Christ makes a Christian what he or she really is. Without Christ we are nothing at all. But with Christ there is no difficulty we cannot overcome.

"Sever all ties, only bind me to you." David Livingston sacrificed his friends, family, health, and possessions for the cause of Christ. We have recorded letters sent back to his family describing the love he felt for them. David Livingston practiced what he preached. As we begin each morning with prayer, we should renew our allegiance to the kingdom of God, putting God first in our lives.

A fitting tribute to Livingston's work is supplied by Stanley:

> I went to Africa as prejudiced as the biggest atheist in London. But there came a long time for reflection. I saw this solitary old man there and asked myself, "How on earth does he stay here? What is it that inspires him?" For months after we met I found myself wondering at the old man carrying out all that was said in the Bible—"Leave all things and follow Me." But little by little my sympathy was aroused; seeing his piety, his gentleness, his zeal, his earnestness, and how he went about his business, I was converted by him, although he had not tried to do it.[1]

Prayer is one means of expressing faith in God. As we see in Livingston's prayer, our time with God should be a recommitment of our lives and a renewing of our fellowship. If Jesus felt it necessary to begin each day in prayer, how much more should you and I!

29

T–Take Time with Your Family

aking time with our families is not based on duty but rather on love. In order to love as God intends, we must love God first. Mark 12:30 says, "And thou shalt love the Lord thy God with all thy heart, and with all thy soul, and with all thy mind, and with all thy strength: this is the first commandment." God's love is a spiritual love. It's not manipulative or possessive. More than anything, it is an unconditional love.

Families are like Christmas trees—the closer the ornaments are to the star, the closer they are to each other. The closer we are to Christ, the closer our family members will be to each other.

Jesus said, "A new commandment I give unto you, That ye love one another; as I have loved you. . . . By this shall all men know that ye are my disciples, if ye have love one to another" (John 13:34–35).

Love's prescription is found in 1 Corinthians 13:4–8. We are to have an unselfish love, one that considers the other person's good rather than our desires. If we truly love our families, we will overcome our selfish natures that often prevent us from spending the time we need. Notice the qualities of true love: it is patient, kind, unselfish, and humble. It is not proud, improper, selfish, or demanding.

Love's produce is the fruit of the Spirit (Gal. 5:22). G. Campbell Morgan related love to these fruits in the following manner:

• Joy is love's consciousness.
• Peace is love's confidence.
• Patience is love's habit.
• Kindness is love's vitality.
• Goodness is love's activity.
• Faithfulness is love's quantity.
• Meekness is love's tone.
• Temperance is love's victory.[1]

Our homes are the proving ground for our faith. When we truly love, these qualities will make us want to spend time together.

Love's power is the Holy Spirit. Romans 5:5 says, "The love of God is shed abroad in our hearts by the Holy Ghost which is given unto us." A man who was struggling in his marriage once said to me, "It all sounds good in theory, but it seems impossible in practice." God will only ask you to do what He equips you to do. However, we must rely on His power and ask for His help. We can learn to love each other because He is the source of love. When God is in control of our lives, love flows in unlimited supply.

30

U–Understand the Basis of Success

In 1923, a very important meeting was held at the Edgewater Beach Hotel in Chicago. Attending this meeting were nine of the world's most successful financiers. Those present were:

- The president of the largest utility company;
- The president of the largest independent steel company;
- The president of the largest gas company;
- The greatest wheat speculator;
- The president of the New York Stock Exchange;
- A member of the President's cabinet;
- The greatest "bear" in Wall Street;
- The head of the world's greatest monopoly;
- The president of the Bank of International Settlements.

There was no doubt this was a gathering of some of the most powerful men in the whole world. But within twenty years look what happened to them:

- The president of the greatest utility company—Samuel Insull—died penniless in a foreign land.
- The president of the largest independent steel company—Charles Schwab—died a bankrupt and lived on borrowed money for five years before his death.

165

- The president of the largest gas company—Howard Hopson—is now insane.
- The greatest wheat speculator—Arthur Cutton—died abroad, insolvent.
- The president of the New York Stock Exchange—Richard Whitney —was sent to the penitentiary.
- The member of the President's cabinet—Albert Fall—was pardoned from prison so he could die at home.
- The greatest "bear" in Wall Street—Jesse Livermore—died a suicide.
- The head of the greatest monopoly—Ivan Krueger—also committed suicide.
- The president of the Bank of International Settlement—Leon Fraser —killed himself.

Unfortunately, some people spend their lives climbing the ladder of success only to find that it's leaning against the wrong wall!

Jesus was the most successful person who ever lived, and He said, "But seek ye first the kingdom of God, and his righteousness; and all these things shall be added unto you" (Matt. 6:33). He made it clear that real success can only be found in seeking the will and purpose of God.

Some people spend their entire lives running away from God and toward His blessings. But the harder they run, the farther away from God they go. If they could only realize that if they turned around and ran toward God, His blessings would follow.

What is success? Money? Fame? Prestige? Possessions? Or is it God, family, righteousness, and truth? Is success something we achieve by merit? Or is it something we receive by grace? Do we earn it by effort? Or receive it by faith? What is your definition of success? Does it square with what Jesus said?

31

V—Value Your Heritage

One day when my son was seven, he came to me and asked that demanding question, "Daddy, where did I come from?" Looking frantically around for help, I realized that it was time for a "birds and bees" talk. Trying to explain it in terms suitable for a second grader, I told him in general about babies. After some of the longest minutes of my life, he looked at me wide-eyed and said, "Wow, Dad, that's interesting! The kid next door said that he came from Florida, and I just wondered where I came from!"

Heritage certainly involves more than your birth. I've been blessed with a wonderful family tree, but I also have a spiritual heritage from my family and church, a political heritage from this great nation, and a social heritage from the area I call home. No one got here on his or her own. We are all the product of our heritage. And that heritage deserves our respect and appreciation.

As a Lee, I am a descendent of Robert E. Lee through my father's side of the family. It is a heritage of which I am both proud and grateful. But as a Christian, I am a spiritual descendent of Christ. As a believer, I'm a child of God. What a heritage we have in Him! It far exceeds any human heritage. It makes us citizens of heaven and brothers and sisters in the family of God.

One of the great examples of spiritual heritage in the Bible is that of the relationship of Elijah and Elisha (2 Kings 2). The venerable old prophet Elijah spent years training young Elisha. When the time of the old prophet's departure came, he left his mantle to his young under-study. It was the symbol of his life and ministry. Passing it on to the next generation was the old prophet's symbolic gesture to his young companion.

But Elisha didn't sit back and admire the mantle. He picked it up and immediately went to work training others. In fact, he reproduced himself in the "sons of the prophets" (his students) more effectively than his predecessor. Why? Because he had a wonderful heritage upon which to build his life and ministry.

And so do you, if you know the Lord! Your spiritual heritage reaches back through faithful preachers, itinerant evangelists, powerful revivalists, courageous pioneers, Pilgrims, Puritans, and Reformers—men and women who risked their lives for the cause of Christ and the gospel. That line of spiritual heritage runs back through time to the days of the martyrs who gave themselves that we might know the truth. That line runs back to Paul's imprisonment, Stephen's stoning, and our Lord's crucifixion. And there it stops—at the foot of the cross!

32

W—Win the Prize

The thrill of victory.

We have all seen the face of an athlete as he or she strains to win a race. Commitment. Determination. Incredible effort. All are necessary to win an athletic contest.

The agony of defeat.

We have also seen the televised images of defeated contestants. Despair. Agony. Rejection. Sometimes it is so unbearable, we can hardly look at it. Nobody wants to lose. But not everybody can win—except in the real game of life.

God is in the business of *turning losers into winners.* Look at our Lord's disciples. They spent three whole years with Him only to forsake, deny, and betray Him in one night. By human standards, they were all losers. But God's grace touched their lives. His Spirit filled them with His power. And they went out and turned the world upside down for God.

God is the ultimate winner. He knows the end from the beginning. Knowing Him puts us in the winner's circle. I'm not talking about going through the outward formalities of religion: joining a church, walking an aisle, making a profession of faith. These may be well and good, but the only way to be truly transformed is from within. Only Christ can change you on the inside so that the difference is seen on the outside.

God loves us so much that He meets us at the point of our needs. When all seems lost, He steps in with the prize in His hand. The victory has already been won. All we have to do is join Him by faith in the winner's circle.

33

X—X-Ray Your Whole Life

X-ray machines are a part of our life. Aside from their medical application, X rays are used extensively in security work. Have you ever wondered what image airport personnel see in your luggage?

"Hmm, nice comb..."

"Why doesn't he clean the coins out of that briefcase?"

"I wonder if she knows that a ring has fallen between the lining and the case?"

I'm sure that they see all kinds of interesting things. But what does God see when He x-rays our lives? The apostle Paul looked back over his life and said, "For I am now ready to be offered, and the time of my departure is at hand. I have fought a good fight, I have finished my course, I have kept the faith: henceforth there is laid up for me a crown of righteousness" (2 Tim. 4:6–8).

We can gain insight into people's lives by reading tombstones. They range from the very factual to the very creative; for example:

- In Dodge City:
> Here lies my wife,
> Here let her lie.
> She's at rest,
> And so am I.

• In England:

> Here lies Johnny Cole,
> Who died, oh my soul,
> After eating a plentiful dinner;
> While chewing his crust,
> He was turned into dust,
> With his crimes undigested—poor sinner!

• In Ireland:

> Within this grave do lie,
> Back to back, my wife and I;
> When the last trump the air shall fill,
> If she gets up, I'll just lie still.

And on the grave of Ben Franklin:

> The Body
> of
> BENJAMIN FRANKLIN
> printer
> (Like the cover of an old book,
> Its contents torn out,
> And stripped of its lettering and gilding)
> Lies here food for worms:
> Yet the work itself shall not be lost,
> For it will, as he believed, appear once more
> In a new
> And more beautiful edition,
> Corrected and amended
> by
> the Author

One of the most moving stories in the Bible is that of Onesimus, a runaway slave. Paul met him in prison, converted him to Christ, and sent him back to Philemon, his master. Instead of running away, he returned to his responsibilities.

But in the process of his return, Paul reminded Philemon that Onesimus was a new man. Onesimus was transformed from slave to brother, from enemy to friend, and from debtor to free man. In the final analysis, when God x-rays our lives, He sees us in light of our relationship to Him.

Fifty years later, on his way to Rome to be martyred, Ignatius wrote of the wonderful Bishop Onesimus. Was he the former runaway slave? He well could have been! For when our whole lives are x-rayed, God doesn't look at what we were in the past but what we are in Christ right now!

34

Y–Yield Yourself Completely

The apostle Paul wrote, "I beseech you therefore, brethren, by the mercies of God, that ye present your bodies a living sacrifice, holy, acceptable unto God, which is your reasonable service" (Rom. 12:1).

Perhaps the biggest obstacle we face in yielding ourself *is* ourself. Someone said that it's hard to present yourself as a sacrifice if you continually crawl off the altar. Most of us are so concerned about ourselves, that we forget to yield ourselves to God.

Three umpires were discussing the way they called balls and strikes:

"I call them the way I see them," said the first umpire.

"I call them the way they are," responded the second.

"They *are* the way I call them," concluded the last.

In God's plan, things are the way He calls them! The sooner we find that out and apply it to our situation, the more yielded we will become to His will.

The story of the prodigal son (see Luke 15:11–24) is one of a young man's resistance to his father's will. A clever paraphrase reads like this:

A Fugitive Found

Feeling footloose and frisky, a featherbrained fellow forced his fond father to fork over the farthings and flew far to foreign fields and frittered his fortune feasting fabulously with faithless friends.

Fleeced by his fellows in folly and facing famine, he found himself a feed flinger in a filthy farm. Fairly famishing, he fain would have filled his frame with foraged food from fodder fragments. "Fooey, my father's flunkies fare far finer!"

The frazzled fugitive forlornly fumbled, frankly facing facts. He fled forthwith to his family. Falling at his father's feet, he forlornly fumbled. "Father, I've flunked and fruitlessly forfeited family."

The farsighted father, forestalling further flinching, frantically flagged the flunkies to fetch a fatling from the flock and fix a feast.

The fugitive's faultfinding brother frowned on fickle forgiveness of the former folderol.

But the faithful father figured, "Filial fidelity is fine, but the fugitive is found! What forbids fervent festivity? Let flags be unfurled! Let fanfares flair!"

It's amazing how quick we are to spot sin in someone else while we excuse sin in our own lives. The prodigal had to admit how bad things had become and turn from his sin. Only then could he yield to his father's wishes.

We can only be completely yielded to God when we consider His cost in forgiveness. The real hero of the parable is the loving father. In addition to the sizable portion of his estate already wasted on the boy, he now gives him a ring, a robe, and a regal roast! Forgiveness always costs. Only when we count the cost of Calvary will we be broken by sin to the point of completely yielding our lives to Him. And, as the prodigal discovered, true fulfillment and happiness are only found in yielding to a loving Father.

35

Z–Zero in Your Ultimate Goal

hat is your ultimate goal? One man said his goal was to live to be one hundred years old "because you rarely ever hear of anyone over one hundred dying!" Others talk of material goals. Martin Luther said, "Riches are the least worthy gifts which God can give man, yet men toil for them day and night, and take no rest. Therefore, God frequently gives riches to foolish people to whom he gives nothing else."[1] Although we can and should set interim goals, they all should work toward our ultimate goal of being one with Christ and His will. Let's see if we can describe our ultimate goal in terms of everyday living.

In His high priestly prayer for all believers (John 17), Jesus prayed for our spiritual *growth*. Growth is evidence of life. Jesus prayed for the inward growth of believers. This inward growth would be easy to measure if, like a child, we could stand next to a wall each year and mark our growth. But inward growth is much more subjective than physical growth. A believer may claim to be twenty years old in the Lord. But have they really grown for twenty years? Or is it one year of growth repeated twenty times? One part of our ultimate goal should be to grow in spiritual maturity like Jesus!

Praying for His small band of disciples, Jesus says, "Neither pray I for these alone, but for them also which shall believe on me through their word" (John 17:20). I don't believe that it's accurate for Christians to say, "God isn't concerned about numbers." There are simply too many numbers recorded in Scripture: He prayed with 3, trained 12, sent out 120, fed 5,000 men, and saw 3,000 saved at Pentecost. Now, somebody had to be concerned enough about numbers to count! Numbers are important in that they represent souls. God is concerned about people, therefore, He is concerned about numbers of people.

Jesus also prayed, "that they all may be one." Unity is not just being in union. Neither is it uniformity. It need not even require unanimity (perfect agreement on all details). Unity flows from our shared purpose as believers: to be like Him and to proclaim His name. We are to do all things for the glory of God. As the world sees Christians united in service, we glorify God. As fellow believers, we must learn to appreciate our differences while not letting them divide our unity. Throughout His prayer, Jesus compares His relationship with the Father as a model for our relationship with Him. He desires a closeness with believers and for believers.

One of the joys of staying at a church for several years is being able to see couples grow together in unity and intimacy. As newly-weds, they're close, but obviously different. Opposites really do attract! It's almost predictable to counsel with a newly married couple and hear their complaints. But, if they stay together and allow God to work out their differences, a deep spiritual and emotional intimacy can be produced. It's delightful to talk to couples who've been married for forty or fifty years. One can often complete the thoughts of the other! They know the faults of their spouse better than anyone else. Yet they allow love to cover those faults. Such is the intimacy Christ desires with His followers. He wants a complete sense of honesty that allows repentance to lead to holiness.

Goals are important. Personal goals. Financial goals. Family goals. But only one goal is ultimate—your eternal relationship to God. It may be closer than you think. Make sure you are ready when He calls. Your future can be secure when it is secure in Jesus Christ.

Notes

Chapter 1
1. Francis Schaeffer, *How Should We Then Live?* (Old Tappan, N.J.: Fleming H. Revell, 1976).
2. George Barna, *Virtual America* (Ventura, Calif.: Regal Books, 1994), 23–32.
3. "Beyond the Year 2000: What to Expect in the New Millennium," *Time* (Special issue, Fall 1992), 10–12.
4. Jan Johnson, "Getting the Gospel to Baby Busters," *Moody* (May 1995), 50.

Chapter 3
1. Stephen Covey, *Seven Habits of Highly Effective People* (New York: Simon & Schuster, 1989), 32.
2. Doug Murren, *Leadershift* (Ventura, Calif.: Regal Books, 1994), 18.
3. Ibid., 28–29.
4. Larry Crabb, *Inside Out* (Colorado Springs: Nav Press, 1988), 23–24.
5. Ibid., 37.
6. Mike Flynn and Doug Gregg, *Inner Healing* (Downers Grove, Ill.: InterVarsity Press, 1993), 18.
7. Ed Young, *Been There. Done That. Now What?* (Nashville: Broadman & Holman, 1994), 7.
8. Octavius Winslow, *Personal Declension and Revival of Religion in the Soul* (Edinburgh: Banner of Truth, 1962 reprint of 1841 original), 14.
9. Patrick Morley, *The Man in the Mirror* (Brentwood, Tenn.: Wolgemuth & Hyatt, 1989), 296–301.

Chapter 4
1. Robert Schuller, *Power Thoughts* (New York: Harper Collins, 1993), 109.

Chapter 5
1. Jack Canfield, "Follow Your Dream," in Jack Canfield and Mark

Hansen, *Chicken Soup for the Soul* (Deerfield Beach, Fla.: Health Communications, 1993), 207–8.

2. Ibid., 219.

3. Chart developed by Edward Hindson, editorial consultant and vice president of *There's Hope!* Atlanta, Georgia.

Chapter 6

1. Walter Wintle, "Thinking," *World's Best Loved Poems* (Harper & Row, 1927).

2. Michael Medved, *Hollywood vs. America* (New York: Harper Collins, 1992), 40–41.

3. "Something Beautiful," words by Gloria Gaither, music by William J. Gaither. © 1971, Wm. J. Gaither, all rights reserved.

4 Jack Hayford, The Power and Blessing (Wheaton, Ill.: Victor Books, 1994), 228.

Chapter 7

1. Russell Conwell, "Acres of Diamonds," quoted in Charles Allen, Victories in the Valleys of Life (Old Tappan, N.J.: Fleming H. Revell, 1981), 74–76.

2. A. M. Overton, quoted in Richard Lee, *The Unfailing Promise* (Dallas: Word Books, 1988), 132–33.

3. Martin Luther, quoted in Ed Hindson and Walter Byrd, *When the Road Gets Rough* (Old Tappan, N.J.: Fleming H. Revell, 1986), 11.

Chapter 8

1. Jon Johnston, *Christian Excellence* (Grand Rapids: Baker, 1985), 154–55.

2. Robert Schuller, *Power Thoughts* (New York: Harper Collins, 1993), 55.

3. R. C. Larson, ed., *The Best of Ted Engstrom* (San Bernardino, Calif.: Here's Life Publishers, 1988), 136–44.

4. Stephen Arterburn, *Winning at Work without Losing at Love* (Nashville: Thomas Nelson, 1994), 191.

5. Helen Steiner Rice, "Prayers Can't Be Answered Unless They Are Prayed," *Gifts from the Heart* (Old Tappan, N.J.: Fleming H. Revell, 1981), 51.

Chapter 9

1. Ed Young, *Been There. Done That. Now What?* (Nashville: Broadman & Holman, 1994), 161–62.

2. Cal Thomas, *The Things That Really Matter* (New York: Harper Collins, 1994), 18ff.

3. Robert Schuller, *Tough Times Never Last, but Tough People Do!* (Nashville: Thomas Nelson, 1983), 57–68.

4. Robert Frost, "The Road Not Taken," *Atlantic Monthly* (August 1915).

Chapter 12

1. Bruce Wilkinson, *Seven Laws of the Learner Seminar,* Walk Through the Bible Ministries.

Chapter 13

1. Gordon W. Prange, *At Dawn We Slept* (New York: McGraw Hill, 1981), 528–29.

2. Loren Eiseley, *The Star Thrower* (New York: Harcourt Brace, 1978), 184.

Chapter 23

1. Winston Churchill, quoted in Michael Green, *Illustrations for Biblical Preaching* (Grand Rapids: Baker, 1982), 185.

2. Ibid.

3. Charles Colson, *A Dangerous Grace* (Dallas: Word Publishing, 1994), 69–70.

Chapter 25

1. Mark McCloskey, *Tell It Often, Tell It Well* (San Bernardino, Calif.: Here's Life Publishers, 1986), 205–6.

2. Tom Hanks, "Would Jesus Stoop to Canned Evangelism?" *Eternity* (Sept. 1973), 24.

Chapter 28

1. Henry M. Stanley, quoted in Walter Knight, ed. *3,000 Illustrations for Christian Service* (Grand Rapids: Eerdmans, 1952), 376.

Chapter 29

1. G. Campbell Morgan, quoted in A. M. Well, *Inspiring Quotations* (Nashville: Thomas Nelson, 1988), 120.

Chapter 35

1. *Lutheran* (April 18, 1979), 3.